PRAISE FOR *HARD TRUTHS*

"Tomlin gets it. In *Hard Truths* each lesson is something most people learn through the school of hard knocks...Leadership isn't something you do, you have to live it!"

SEN. MARV HAGEDORN
U.S. Navy Mustang (Retired)

"In *Hard Truths*, Dr. Michael Tomlin vividly illustrates and exemplifies how you can transform your work experiences into business building blocks. Each chapter offers a quick read about how those building blocks set a solid foundation for successful business leadership. You'll pause after each chapter of *Hard Truths* to recall similar experiences that you can utilize to empower your employees to increase productivity."

RICK CARPENTER
Managing Editor, The Sumter Item

"I love this book. *Hard Truths* is an essential book for all business leaders! It is full of practical information in an easy-to-read format. This book would have been especially beneficial to me in my early life as a business manager."

DR. LINDA REID
Emeritus Professor of Business

"*Hard Truths: 18 Rock-Solid Lessons for Leaders* by Michael Tomlin is rock solid! This book is packed with insights into 18 different leadership topics that leaders need to understand to be efficient and effective. This book was an easy read—I love the fact that I can now refer to specific sections to brush up on a particular topic. The stories and humor makes the messages very memorable. This is a must-read for all leaders and those who are wanting to become leaders."

LIZ HENSLEY, PHD
City Councilor, Alamosa, CO
Professor and MBA Director, Adams State University

"This distillation of leadership principles is reflective of the best that we know, and will withstand the test of time. Dr. Tomlin has provided a concise overview of the essentials of leadership success, while blending his decades of experience throughout. *Hard Truths* is an enjoyable reminder of what is critically important in working with people and organizations."

TRAVIS FREDERICKSON
President and CEO, C4 Practice Services

"*Hard Truths* is a quick and enjoyable read. Mike Tomlin's concept of authenticity is spot-on. The idea that resonated the most with me was in the 'Focus' chapter. It is so easy to get fixated on small mistakes and miss larger ones, or simply fail to recognize when something is right, because you are looking for your 'pet' mistake. I plan to use that concept with my management team at our next meeting. Thanks for sharing."

NATHAN CHERPESKI
City Manager, Klamath Falls, OR

"Grit! I've seen movies about it, sandpaper is measured by it; but how long has it been since grit was a necessary trait in true leaders? The short answer is that the attribute became unfashionable with the dumbing down of this great country. Instead of grit, we promote traits like compromise and compassion, both very admirable qualities with balance. In *Hard Truths*, Michael Tomlin suggests that if we once again want to be the country regarded as the best in the world, we're going to have to admit what it takes to get there. Grit is just one of the many missing hard truths we must regain to do so."

RANDY WRIGHT
Executive Director, Alamosa County Economic
Development Corporation

"I absolutely love this book–it's an easy, quick read. The *Hard Truths* are very important to understand, but have not always been obvious. I myself have bought into the wrong ideas and behavior about burnout and balance. I also suffered a major career setback because I failed to recognize the crucial importance of fitting into a company's culture. Thanks for explaining truths that so many of us have to learn the hard way."

ALLISON STALEY
Director/VP of Sales and Marketing, Stafit LLC

HARD
TRUTHS

18 ROCK-SOLID LESSONS FOR LEADERS

MICHAEL TOMLIN

elevate

M. Tomlin
1351 E. Ashbrook Dr.
Eagle, ID 83616

To Kenton,
a fellow educator,
thinker, and
leader.

and a friend.

Keep on!

Mike

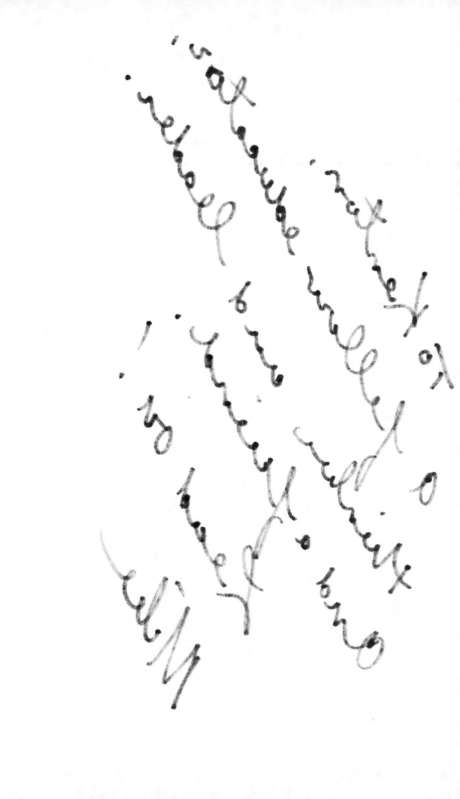

DEDICATION

First and foremost, this book is dedicated to my late father who, without a college degree, taught me about business and people in nearly every conversation we had. Called from Kansas into World War II, and working two jobs much of my childhood, he never complained. He worked, he provided, and he was always proud of my mother, my sister, and me.

Secondly, I dedicate this book to the Infantry School at Fort Benning, Georgia, where I received my officer training and commission, and to the many outstanding leaders of all ranks and branches I served with in the United States Army.

I further dedicate it to those I have worked for, with, and adjacent to in civilian life who are intelligent and caring, work inspired, and who make/made a difference in their organizations. I learned from some of the best.

Finally, I dedicate this book to those others I learned from. The incompetent, the self-serving, the unethical, the uninspired, and the whiners—I learned from them too.

And thus this book.

TABLE OF CONTENTS

ACKNOWLEDGMENTS

First, I want to thank Elevate Publisher Mark Russell for believing in this book, and the entire staff for helping to shepherd it into this form. I also acknowledge and thank Maryanna Young of Aloha Publishing, who liked the book idea but helped refer it (and me) to the best fit for my publishing needs.

I acknowledge and thank Anna McHargue, for her editing efforts in getting the right words *rightly* on the page and for believing in the book from the beginning. I also thank final editor Jana Good who, among other contributions, is responsible for the proper insertion of at least 200 commas, something that I generally don't find useful.

And, of course, I acknowledge and thank my wonderful wife, Sue, and my family for their support during the ups and downs of my career and throughout the writing of this book.

1

AUTHENTICITY

You must live it to lead by it

———

My search for authenticity began with my search for a martial arts instructor. I was near 50 years old living in Boise, Idaho, where dozens of martial arts studios and instructors dotted the strip malls. I visited most. Most were prepared to teach me in the Asian traditions that I desired, but finding an instructor who taught and lived the martial "way" was altogether different. I could sign up and learn what I have come to call "sneaky Asian fighting," but I wanted much more.

Then I found it—a small studio with an eclectic collection of students and a teacher who slept on a rice mat on the floor of his studio. Czech by birth, American by choice, he taught both the fighting techniques and the "way." Unlike some martial artists, who were merely technique stylists, Kossi wanted us to care about and learn the "way." He was as authentic as he advertised, as he delivered, and as he lived.

"…martial arts is not what you do,
but rather how you live." (paraphrased)

—Forrest E. Morgan, *Living the Martial Way (1992)*

The same holds true with leaders. Our teams notice our authenticity. They notice what we say, what we do, and how we live. They notice if their doctor smokes. They notice if their nutritionist is overweight. They notice the charity of their pastor. They notice us in the office, on the phone, online, with other employees, with clients or customers, and they notice nonstop. In 1983, English rock band The Police (Sting) recorded and scored the No. 1 song of the year, "Every Breath You Take." While the hit song has some unfortunate stalking overtones, the message was clear: "Every move you make, every breath you take, I'll be watching you." That is a perfect lesson for leaders, especially those who wish to be seen as authentic. Our employees, our faculty, our troops, our department, our work teams, our clients, and our customers are watching us.

In 2015 (January), *Harvard Business Review* proudly proclaimed, "Authenticity has become the gold standard for leadership." Of course it has, which likely explains why we see our political leaders as so very authentic. (Well, maybe not so much.) But if there were an authenticity scale, most of us would like to be rated as more so, rather than less so.

Those who read leadership books regularly are sure to have noticed that "authentic" has become one of those buzzwords publishers can sink their teeth into…a real winner when it comes to selling books. Authenticity is the new secret sauce. But how do we become more authentic, and a more authentic leader? We do so by *being* it and rejecting the myriad multi-step programs, assessments, and buzzwords offered by so many.

If we can accept a standard dictionary definition of authentic, then the path becomes clear. The challenges remain, but that is what this book is about. Let's look at *Merriam-Webster. com*:

Authentic: real or genuine; true and accurate; not false, copied, or imitation; worthy of acceptance; true to one's own personality, spirit, or character.

Easy enough. But leadership books too often don't like definitions. In *Authentic Leadership* (Bill George, 2003), which is credited with pioneering the idea of authentic leadership, the author lists "leading with the heart" as one of "five qualities" of the authentic leader. That might be true and accurate for a heart-driven leader, but not at all real or genuine for a mission-focused, budget-driven leader who might be extremely authentic—just not a "heartful" kind of gal or guy. There is the rub. There can be no five qualities, six characteristics, seven traits, or any other numbered list of authenticity classifiers. You are, or you are not. Having said that, authenticity is never a guarantee of good (or poor) leadership. My point is simply that there is a difference between *"I am Batman,"* and *"I do Batman things, as shown by my score on a Batman scale."*

Few of us are Batman. We are who we are, and can become who we wish to become if we care sufficiently about it. In Hard Truth #7, "Intentionality," we take this theme a good step further. For now, let's look at our authenticity in a real and practical leadership manner.

Understand that we don't lead in a certain manner because "they" are watching, but rather we behave as we are and assume or even hope they are watching. That is how we teach and grow our employees, and establish and reinforce relationships with them and their customers. While sometimes it is hard to show exact examples of authenticity, it is easy to show poor ones—behave a certain way day in and day out and then conduct a training session and teach a different behavior to your team, or hold a staff meeting and demand different actions by your subordinates than what you model daily. (Hard Truth #4, "The 'M' Factor: Mission, Message, and Motivation Must Match," establishes a strong foundation for consistent messaging.)

Nowhere does the "authenticity flag" wave higher than in the practices and rituals you put into place in your organization. The ones you model, you display, you teach, and you reward. If there is a mission statement on the wall, then the authentic leader speaks of it daily in routine conversations. It's not something forced or contrived, or something the team has to remember to do. Rather, it is DNA to them. They understand it is why they were hired and what they are paid to do. Thus, it becomes part of their common rituals. They are it, and it is them. BAM! Batman!

In the book *The Four Agreements* (1997), Don Miguel Ruiz shares insights into Toltec wisdom, the Toltecs having a better grasp on authenticity than many contemporary leadership writers. The first "agreement" is that you will be "impeccable with your word." Sounds easy; simply don't lie, and always tell the truth. But that doesn't get you close. The word "impeccable" implies without sin. Suddenly, that is a higher standard.

Think of a person who is well-dressed, and then think of them impeccably dressed. Those are indeed two very different standards. I would argue the authentic leader would set a personal standard to be impeccable with their word, and then live and work in a manner that would continually narrow the gap between any failings in their word and impeccability. It is not something for them to "do," but rather, part of what they wish to become.

No, the authentic leader is not one who follows steps or checks authenticity boxes on an assessment instrument or scale. They are authentic unto themselves. They lead authentic lives, and, as such, are authentic to others. They are executives, managers, directors, or emerging leaders who understand the rules of Sting, and desire to become Batman. Both are attainable, but you must *be* what you want your business to become.

HARD TRUTH #1:

AUTHENTIC LEADERSHIP ONLY COMES FROM AUTHENTIC PEOPLE WHO LIVE AUTHENTIC LIVES.

HARD TRUTH #2

BALANCE

Leaders are never overwhelmed;
they manage and they lead

I stood in the open door of the C-123 aircraft as it came up from its below-the-radar safety at treetop level to just under 1,000 feet elevation (above ground level) and saw the green light by the door light up. The jumpmaster, with one last look outside the door, swung his arm and pointed downward through the door and yelled, "Go!" I jumped and tucked into the midnight sky with the rest of my team behind me, counting steadily and feeling the reassuring snap of my parachute inflating with a jerk, then concentrated on steering the chute through the night sky to our landing point. One by one, all members of the team landed, rolled their chutes, rallied, buried the chutes, and moved quickly through the mountains. So far, so good.

Several days later, while taking a short break from our reconnaissance mission and checking our map location with my team sergeant, I asked him, "You know what I would really like right now?" He looked up and raised his eyebrows in question. "Some work/life balance," I said. He snorted and smiled just as I nodded that it was time to move. "Saddle up," he told the men.*

All of the above is true, except for what I told my team sergeant. We had never heard of work/life balance. Work was work and life was life. Similarly for my father who, with the exception of a few short years, always worked two jobs, work was work. He provided for us, loved us, and never complained. Take a job, do the job. Never speak ill of those you take money from. He was a company man.

Not so with much of the workforce today, so it caught my attention big time back in 2004 when the October cover of *Fast Company* screamed "Balance is Bunk!" Yes, finally, honesty.

And, here's some more honesty: "Burnout" is bunk as well.

We work hard today, we live easy or hard today, and we do it over and over. The *Fast Company* piece, certainly still worthy of reading, began by portraying a "week that defied sanity." We've all had them. The article notes a week with an impossible deadline at work, scheduled school or athletic events with your kids, car trouble, cranky spouse, cranky self, and a new project dumped in your lap.

The article's authors (Keith Hammond, Michael Aneiro, et al.) correctly drilled down to the secret core of balance and burnout happiness, and discovered these are simply problems of logistics and economics. We're the managers. We're the leaders. We should be able to manage logistics and economics! Your car is broken? Deliver it or have it picked up by the dealer or shop, take a loaner or rent one, and move forward. Spouse cranky? Send them (unexpectedly) some nice flowers or a bottle of scotch, new golf balls, or whatever they like, with a note expressing your love and an apology for being distracted. Too many scheduled school events? Cut them in half and double down on your work, nailing the projects that will provide the income to support your kids' schooling and activities. Don't look back and don't regret.

I live not far from a stretch of the Oregon Trail. Whenever I feel a bit too extended, I think of the pioneers, settling the Northwest, day in and day out on the trail. Hardship. Loss. Tragedy. Burnout? No. Looking for balance? No, they were moving in a direction of their dreams. How about me? Or you? Before we complain about burnout, we should check and make certain we were ever on fire…and then stoke it and add fuel. Let it become the fire in our belly.

How many hours did we think it would take to raise children? To keep a fulfilling marriage? To make partner at the firm? To earn tenure at the university? To grow our own start-up from scratch? There are 168 hours in a week; the rest is logistics and economics. Thank you, *Fast Company*!

The late Stephen Covey—author of *The 7 Habits of Highly Effective People*—famously said that few people on their deathbed wished they had spent more time in the office. Point taken. And Covey's book has been a huge addition to leadership literature, and helped influence my thinking and development in my career. However, this statement was made after Covey had earned his money, which made things easier for him to make the point.

I was sitting in a seminar taught by "The World's Greatest Salesman." I know he was because the flyer said so and the seminar fee reinforced it. But he was well-known and promised to offer a lot. At the end, he entertained questions from the audience, and one person asked for the *real* secret. What made him special? How did he *really* outsell his coworkers? His answer was simple: "When the last person in the office goes home, I make five more calls." Of course he does. Logistics and economics. He works the phones and invests more time.

Caroline Dowd-Higgins, writing for *The Huffington Post* (07/08/2015), reinforces her view that balance is bunk and offers a selection of strategies for a more realistic work life. Two strong strategies include: 1) single-tasking, and 2) calendaring. Many workers proclaim skill and success with multitasking, but recent studies have shown they too often sacrifice quality and time with any given project. Thus, they end up churning numerous projects at a time and finishing few. (More about that in Hard Truth #5, "Time.")

To ensure you are using your 168 hours effectively, the practice and discipline of managing a calendar is critical. Schedule your sleep; schedule your family's major events; schedule your time in the gym or church, or on your bike; schedule your clients, work team meetings, and planning and project time. Then expect to hold discipline to the majority of that time. Part of discipline is not being coerced to intrude on scheduled time. Only three things should ever *force* a change to your calendar:

1. Direction from a senior boss

2. A time-sensitive critical issue with a client

3. A family emergency

Other issues are scheduled in open slots, and your feeling of burnout begins to go away.

Good leaders are never overwhelmed, but they may be fully whelmed...

Learning to manage your work when you are fully whelmed is part of your maturation as an effective leader. When I was a young army lieutenant, I remarked to an older and far more experienced senior sergeant about an upcoming assignment, "Sergeant Daly, this is not going to be easy." He gently replied, "Sir, if it was a lesser mission they would have assigned it to lesser men." Point taken. What kind of leader did I wish to become? Needless to say, there was no discussion about work-life balance or burnout.

A story is told about a crew of men building a railroad in the early western (U.S.) expansion days. The men were swinging their sledges and driving spikes. One of them looked up and saw the private car of the railroad president coming up the track. It stopped, and off the back of the shiny private car stepped the president, surveying the work and the crew and lighting a cigar.

One of the spike drivers yelled to him, "Hey, Russ!" The president looked, then yelled back, "Jim! Come over here." The crewman jogged over to the president, and they shook hands and visited. After a short while, they shook hands again and the crewman jogged back. The other men were aghast. "You know him. The president of this railroad?" they all asked. "Oh, yes," replied Jim. "He and I started out here 10 years ago driving spikes."

"So what happened?" they all clamored. "How come you are here and he is the president?" Jim slowly answered, "Well, I went to work for $10 a week, and he went to work for the railroad."

So, go to work for a firm or start your own. Set your priorities and manage your 168 hours weekly. Show your talent, make your mark, and don't regret. Ever.

HARD TRUTH #2:

BALANCE AND BURNOUT ARE BUNK.

*Note: The author served in the United States Army Airborne from 1968-1985, with active and reserve service. He was attached to both the 12th and 19th Special Forces (Airborne) Groups, serving as an operational detachment (ODA) commander and company operations and training officer (S3), achieving the rank of major prior to honorable discharge.

CULTURE

Work where you fit, and hire people who fit

———

The trainer was teaching us about race relations. He was sent from corporate headquarters, and everyone in our regional branch office sat in attendance. We were a good group with good attitudes and a good relationship with corporate. I found myself not buying the trainer's message. I wondered if my coworkers weren't either. The message was adverse to my core beliefs. This was not good.

Following the several-hour training, we bid the trainer farewell as he left for the airport to fly home. We all looked at each other, considering whether or not to discuss the training. We did, and none of us agreed with the trainer or corporate's position. But we discussed it and ultimately decided to send a message up the flagpole that we had concerns and questions. I was senior (in rank) and it fell to me to write the message. I wrote a position paper questioning the message we had just heard, shared it with our team, and, with their concurrence, sent it to corporate.

I was placed on administrative leave the next week, and fired shortly thereafter. Ouch. This was not good—mid-career and out of work. In retrospect, I should have known. I am a so-cial scientist and pride myself on understanding organizations and their culture. It was clear that I was the one who didn't fit.

I had left good work for this position and I liked it, a lot. But somehow I knew I was a forced fit for the culture. I was okay with that, but not okay enough to stay silent when my core beliefs collided with those of the organization. As I said, this one was on me. When it comes to organizational culture, the organization gets to be right.

The truth is that this scenario should probably happen more often than it does. Far too often when conducting train-ings, I hear employees speak ill of the direction of their orga-nization—not just about products or services, but rather the cultural underpinnings of the company. The bottom line is that if you do not have some level of passion around, or support for, your company's culture and values, neither will you sell pas-sionately for them—nor will you create, build, design, or lead with passion. You will find yourself tied to the money, your house, and your community, but not your firm. The bottom line here is that the firm underperforms. Firms deserve better when they pay our salaries.

Organizational culture is defined as shared values, beliefs, traditions, philosophies, and rules. And the organization gets to define each of those unless they violate our civil or other legal rights.

We mainly find situations of non-fitting employees due to poor hiring practices. Companies advertise badly, and then in-terview badly. To find fit we need to advertise for fit, and then interview and select for fit. Assuming competent skills, *fit* is the most important decision we make when hiring personnel.

For example, if a Baptist church is looking for a preacher, they do not just advertise for a preacher. He or she will need to be a Baptist first, and then hopefully want to pastor this church and this congregation in this town. But being a Baptist is foremost.

So it is with other organizations. I liken their culture to a religious denomination. The organizational "denomination" of Apple is different than that of HP, Microsoft, Walmart, or General Motors. All are great companies, but extremely different to work for. And just like marriage, where some people are a better "fit" than others, so it is with employment. There is a right firm for you and me, likely numerous ones. There also are wrong firms. Wrong firms and wrong organizations for the wrong people. And sometimes wrong communities.

As an acquaintance related to me a few years ago, he had recently accepted a teaching position in a medium-sized school district. He was lamenting how difficult it was because the community was very conservative and the school board even more so. That made it difficult for him to teach the children as he wished. He was "forced" to use certain curricular materials, forced to teach to certain standards, and forced to prepare the children for success on standardized tests. "It's just all wrong," he told me. Maybe. But when I asked him why he accepted a teaching position in the most conservative community in one of the most conservative states (Idaho) in the United States, he didn't have an answer. It just never occurred to him that it would matter. He left that teaching position, and both he and the school district were happier. More importantly, both could then be more productive as they wished.

It matters that we do the work we are paid to do in the manner in which we are directed, and for the outcomes the executives or governing boards have decided. A good match between us and corporate DNA allows the leadership to maintain the culture the organization wants. If that doesn't work, we simply move to another firm or start our own.

Disneyland is the happiest place on earth. It says so on the sign in front of the park, and the company famously hires to keep it that way. Attending a leadership conference hosted by Disney execs some years ago, I learned how Disney maintains that culture. They hire happy people. During interviewing they pay little attention to the answers given by the candidate but great attention to their face—do they smile, laugh easily, have twinkling eyes, and make eye contact? Job applicants were informed that keeping Disneyland the happiest place on earth is job No. 1. Selling tickets, working concessions, etc.—all of that is job No. 2.

Imagine that same school district I previously referenced advertising for this teacher:

> Wanted: Energetic and committed history teacher to teach historical foundations of America and its traditional values. Responsibilities include utilizing District curricular materials and ensuring each student achieves proficiency level in end-of-course standardized exams.

Rather than:

> Wanted: history teacher. Must hold state certification in secondary social studies.

Here, the second job posting says nothing. In the first, the school district has been clear in what it wants and expects, and applicants can apply or not based upon that knowledge. It is interesting how clear the job and expectations are in Montessori schools, yet how vague and unclear they can be in public schooling and, truthfully, in many companies and organizations. You never just want an accountant or engineer; you want one that will fit your firm. Your firm has a "denomination." Use it.

I understand and appreciate that it is difficult to hire as we want without running afoul of the Americans with Disabilities Act, or other civil and employment rights laws. If our firm's culture is that we take noon breaks and play volleyball, we can't hire only volleyball-playing people. But, in such an example, it is not volleyball that is the culture, but rather play, fitness, teamwork, or camaraderie. Most employees can contribute and be part of the team without physically playing, and without feeling left out or intimidated. Advertise and interview for this type of culture, and the right applicants will emerge.

Two companies that hire for their culture are Patagonia and Hobby Lobby. Both have directly focused core beliefs and values as companies, and both have fiercely loyal workers committed to the "way" and not just the job. They are great examples of how culture can be done right. Not contrived. Not forced or argued, but DNA-deep in those who work there. In great companies, if you manage the culture well, you will have managed the corporation well also.

As for me, I moved on successfully from the setback that began this chapter. But not perfectly, or forever. I continue to learn that life is full of lessons and we should savor them along the way.

HARD TRUTH #3:

YOU MUST ADVERTISE FOR, INTERVIEW, HIRE, REWARD, AND PROMOTE EMPLOYEES WHO WILL SUPPORT AND PERPETUATE THE ORGANIZATIONAL CULTURE THAT YOU WANT.

THE "M" FACTOR

Mission, Message, and Motivation Must Match

―――――――

"Why won't employees simply follow our mission? They went to the training. It's posted on the wall and printed on the back of their business cards, for crissake." It was a fair question, and asked by a frustrated young manager who was obviously tired of hearing me wax on about missions and mission statements. It was early in the day's workshop and the answer would have been clear by mid-afternoon. But he asked it now, not knowing he would dislike the answer more than he disliked his employees not being mission-followers.

"Because you teach them not to," I replied simply, raising my hand to acknowledge his coming protest and then explaining the point. After my explanation, he understood and grudgingly accepted that his management team's practices actually undercut the very mission they desired to support. This understanding came not because I am smart and he is not, but rather because I have studied and worked with many organizations and have the trained, sharp, outside eyes to view his practices. It is why I was hired—to fix the slippage between effort and productivity in their company. The caveat is, of course, that trainers don't fix things, but sometimes we can observe and suggest tweaking practices to improve a process.

I told this manager it was likely his management messages, routines, and incentives were not totally aligned with the mission. Thus, the employees received mixed messages. In such cases, they almost always default to their manager's most recent message rather than to the mission statement hanging on the wall.

I call it the *"M"* Factor.

MISSION, MESSAGE, & MOTIVATION MUST MATCH

In its simplest form, if your mission calls for perfect customer service and all of your staff meetings are about reducing staff and overtime, which message do you expect employees to hear? Management personnel can often walk that tightrope, but don't expect your employees to. They will default to what you last told them, or what you last reprimanded them for, or what you last paid them a bonus for, or the directives that keep coming from the corporate office—more sales, higher margins, and cut costs and personnel.

Increased sales, higher margins, and cost cutting are hardly new. Let's expect such edicts from higher up, but your job as a manager is to not let those constant messages override the message of your mission. You must make it just as constant. Understand that your mission is stuck on a plaque on the wall, captive to the frame and glass that encapsulates it and the adhesive that keeps it immobile. Who, if not you, advocates for it in meetings, telephone calls, emails, and any and all conversations? Doing that is the leadership difference.

To make that difference, start with rituals and routines. Think for a moment how many conversations—short or long—you have per day with each employee you supervise, regularly interact with, or otherwise have the opportunity to influence. Now, how many of those conversations generally contain aspects of your mission? In uniformed services and sports, the number can be high, but in business and governmental organizations, the answer is often zero.

This is your opening. You're the manager. Begin to infuse micro statements of your mission in conversations; begin and end all staff meetings with such statements. Start making those statements into the conversations employees hear and remember the most.

Think metaphor. In church, they begin and end services and meetings with prayer. What is your metaphoric equivalent to infuse your desired mission messages into the work meetings? Rotarians (Rotary International) begin their meetings with their "Four-way Test," and the military exchanges the hand salute between different ranks of personnel. None of these are magic formulas for success; rather, they are rituals and routines, constant reminders of the things each organization holds as a high truth.

Employees notice where and how you spend your time. They notice your rituals and routines, or lack thereof. And they notice what you reinforce (or not) in daily conversations. Your effort can be as simple as:

> "Jane, I know I'm asking you to watch your team's overtime hours. But let's agree we're not going to sacrifice customer service—exemplary service is our mission—

but be as strategic as you can with scheduling and staff-
ing and see if you can bring those overtime costs down.
Talk to your team, but keep service foremost in their
minds. Let me know what you need from me…except,
of course, more money [laughter], we know where we
are there."

Operating capital needs can indeed be an operating reality.
Organizations must have the money to service their mission.
But talented and skilled managers can truly schedule and staff
more strategically than those less so. Even as you can expect
your managers to develop and carry out those strategies, don't
expect them all to possess the right language to work with their
subordinates.

That is why it is important to role-play with them, toss-
ing in the right words and phrases to give them the tools they
should expect from you. These won't be words that you just
made up or pulled out of the seat of your pants. You will have
selected these words and phrases with intentionality (more on
that in Hard Truth #7). They will be the perfect words and
phrases that you want them to use, over and over, to provide
the message and motivation that will support and serve your
mission. That is mentoring. That is leadership.

Before long, messaging and motivation will be noticeably
supporting the mission. The mission will no longer be lonely
on the wall, huddled behind the glass frame; that young manager I referenced earlier will not be wondering why employees
won't follow it.

Your job, then, is to ensure proper recognition for their ultimate achievement. When bonuses or awards are handed out,
verbally recognize maintaining high service during low fund-
ing rather than awarding for cost cutting. Proper recognition is

authentic to your mission, and will reinforce all that you have been saying and modeling.

Ultimately, it is important to understand that motivated, mission-focused, collaborative, empowered, productive workforces or teams don't just happen. These working environments are created, arranged, crafted, put together, built, established, and assigned; they are fed, cared for, maintained, cultivated, and motivated...they are the product of intelligent design. Yours, if you're ready for the ride.

HARD TRUTH #4:

EMPLOYEES DO WHAT YOU MOTIVATE THEM TO DO, NOT WHAT YOUR MISSION SAYS.

TIME

Time is a currency—it is what you spend to accomplish things

———

The trainer said it again. "There are no B's, each task is either an A or a C." We were hard-pressed to understand his point. There had to be B's if there were A's and C's. The speaker was an efficiency expert, hired to help us with our time management.

Trying again, he slowed down and made it clear. "Any job or task you do not get done today that will result in you being fired, demoted, or reprimanded, is an A. And any job or task you do not get done today that will *not* result in you being fired, demoted, or reprimanded, is a C." Then we got it—one either must get a task done today, or not. That is why there are no B's.

The trainer's reasoning made sense then, and it makes sense now. He had us label each document with a large A or C, then place it in corresponding drawers in our desks. That was in the late 1970s. What a difference computers, smartphones, spreadsheets, task lists, and project management and scheduling software have made. They have given us no more time, but we can plan and audit our spending of it like never before.

Pretty much every philosopher since language was invented has taught us that the one fair thing in life is time. We all get the same amount. We all have an auto-filling account of 24 hours per day, 168 hours each week. We cannot say, "Sure, Mark Zuckerberg invented Facebook, but he had 32 hours a day. Anyone could have done it with 32 hour days." Nope. He got 24, just like the rest of us.

And that auto-filling account has automatic deductions taken out of it—eat, sleep, toilet, commute to work and home, family and civic responsibilities, and, oh yes, work itself. People can easily end up with their schedules looking like their credit card statements—out of control with debt piling each month.

But we should be better. Time is not new. For each of us, time is like personal finance. There are people who make the same amount of money, but some are always broke and some are comfortable. Time may be our highest value currency. It is what we spend to get work done. We don't spend our knowledge, talent, ambition, or drive; those are things we get to keep. But time winds down to zero each deadline day, whether we accomplish our work or not. We have an exact, predictable, finite amount of time for each project or task, and better managers spend it better.

We cannot save time, harness time, or bottle time. It is fruitless to complain about not enough time, because we all get our newly replenished 24 hours every day at midnight. It is spent based upon the choices we have made and continue to make. What we can do is make plans and schedules, and hold discipline to those. We can order our lives and control some of the time wasters and time distractors. Legendary Japanese swordsman, painter, and writer Miyamoto Musashi (1584-1645) makes it seem easy in his *Book of Five Rings*. He lists nine ways to order your life, and ends with "do not perform useless acts." Exactly. They take time and gain nothing.

Yahoo CEO Marissa Meyer reflected on her early days helping to build Google (*Bloomberg Businessweek* 08/04/2016) and her famous 130-hour workweeks. "If you're strategic about when you sleep, when you shower, and how often you go to the bathroom," Meyer said, "then you can accomplish a great deal in short order." So it is with time; like any currency, you invest a lot when you expect to get a lot. From all-night college study sessions before finals, to attorneys prepping major cases, to the Google development team, and for all of us in between, time ticks. We invest it with the courage and strategy of leaders, or we let it control us and we live with excuses, regret, and time debt piling up.

Given that extreme schedules are not sustainable long term for most of us, it is important to develop time-spending strategies that can result in great achievements, such as Google. Just don't waste time doing useless things. The useless things can become very comfortable "standard deductions" of time, just like with taxes. But unlike with tax, reducing our wasted or useless time deductions gives us more time for intentional spending.

When I was a university professor of business, my currency of time was allocated into 50-minute class periods for each class I taught. That's all the university "purchased" for me to teach the students a particular class and subject. It spent down frighteningly fast, and there was no replenishing it. I either took the students to the required level of knowledge and skill by the end of a semester—or I did not. Either way, the time budget was on me. It could be well spent (invested) or mostly frittered away. Regardless, at semester end it was gone.

To go back to the training scenario that began this chapter, a big problem with time is that research shows workers work on what they enjoy most. How does that impact those A's and C's? Add to that the continual call for a more European work schedule, a shorter workday, or four-day workweek. Dan Ariely, writing for *The Wall Street Journal* (07/23/2016), shows the problems with this. Whatever our time on the job, let's accept that some time is wasted. If that is the time we reduce, writes Ariely, then a shortened work time would be fine; but what if those reduced hours "come at the expense of our most productive time?"

In addition to calls for shorter days, we live in an era when discussions of "quality time" and wanting to "have it all" abound. The hard truth is that there is no such thing as quality or non-quality time. Life is life, work is work, and time is time; the clock keeps ticking, it doesn't care. So, we remember the words of the philosophers and look to invest our time wisely, while enjoying every minute.

Some of us are early risers, productive in the morning, and some of us are bats, with our most productive time late at night. I am the former; 4 a.m. is fine with me. In the office by 6 a.m., I can knock out power work before the craziness hits. Others get the kids to bed at 9 p.m. and then hit it hard until after midnight. The most productive writing team I have ever known went to bed early, then got up at 1 a.m. to write. We all have our ways, but we cannot think we are tricking or defeating time. Time will win.

Ultimately, our use of time is bigger than merely not wishing to be fired, demoted, or reprimanded...and separating our A's from our C's. Because many of us want to create and build, our desires help us manage our time. We simply withdraw a number of minutes or hours from our 168-hour weekly allotment and invest what is necessary for our creation. And we never look back or regret.

HARD TRUTH #5:

TIME WON'T WAIT AND TIME DOESN'T CARE. SUCCESSFUL PEOPLE ORDER THEIR LIVES INTENTIONALLY AND MAKE TIME IRRELEVANT.

PAY

Proper pay intersects with ambition, talent, and value

———

M y colleague walked into my office, sat down, and said, "I'm not happy with our merit raises." I was taken aback because we were the same rank, had the same longevity in the state organization, and both understood that merit raises were never very large. While mine was satisfying, I soon learned my colleague's was not.

Part of his unhappiness, it turned out, stemmed from my raise. It was larger than his, and he told me in detail what a good year he had had. There was little I could comment. I, too, had a good year, received the raise, and kept working. I never thought to be satisfied or not based upon others' raises, because I never looked to see what anyone else received. Because we worked for a state agency and the information was public, my colleague had researched it for the sake of comparison. He determined that I was the reason he didn't get a larger raise.

It is interesting, yet should not be surprising, how people compare their pay. First, pay voyeurism is indicative of a larger worldview. People are either *inner-driven* or *other-driven*, meaning they direct their lives based upon internal drivers or they direct their lives based upon external comparisons—the old "keeping up with the Joneses" mentality. I am the former, and my colleague the latter.

Inner-driven people set and adjust what they must have out of life by their needs and their desires and ambitions. They know their talent and time investments will get them where they expect to go, or, of course, they may just not make it. Either way, it is up to them. It is how our economy, workplace, and society work. It is a cool thing.

Inner-driven: Pay = ambition + talent + value

Other-driven people certainly have needs and desires, but they audit those externally based upon peer groups or targeted comparator individuals. Their assessments of success relate to their vertical achievements when compared with those other groups or individuals. So it is with their pay.

Other-driven: Pay (should) = talent + contribu-
tions normed with peer comparisons

In management, we generally know our market value. We know what other similar organizations pay, and we know whether or not we are where we "should" be. Ultimately, if we are not satisfied, we can blame others or step up our game and add more value to our contributions, provided we have the ambition and talent.

With workers (i.e., those not in management), however, it is different. They often do not know their market value, have fewer options, and simply rely on those of us in management to treat them fairly. But what is fairly? Compensation software company PayScale surveyed 71,000 employees to get a feeling of how well or poorly workers think they are being paid. The study, in the *Harvard Business Review* (December 2015), gave almost scary insights into worker perceptions of their pay. Scary—but not surprising.

The study revealed that only 30 percent of employees who were paid at the market rate believed they were being paid fairly, and an incredible 64 percent believed they were underpaid. Even more insightful is that 35 percent of employees who were paid *above* the market rate believed they were underpaid, and 45 percent believed they were paid fairly. It is heartening to know that 20 percent of workers who were paid above market rates recognized that fact.

It is less heartening to understand that overpaid workers seldom provide "overpaid" level contributions, and those who perceive themselves underpaid tend to underperform. Frederick Herzberg's classic study, commonly known today as the two-factor theory, cites the role of pay in employee motivation. Increased pay does not result in increased motivation, but lower pay may result in decreased motivation. Herzberg also concluded that the work itself is sometimes the best motivator, especially for those who believe work is a natural and proper expenditure of time and effort.

What we learn from all of this is that money is a direct motivating factor only for those who are motivated by money—commissioned sales employees, partners in firms where profits are shared, managers who are in a bonus structure, or people who move from job to job for higher pay. Rank-and-file workers will desire a pay raise, but when it comes, they tend to believe they were already due the raise. Since raises are rarely very large, the organization gains little from the effort. At best, employees maintain preexisting levels of motivation and performance.

This is not to say that management does not or should not give raises when it is the right thing to do. If we want to be known as a company or organization that treats workers with appreciation and respect, then our pay policies should reflect the same. We will never regret treating good people well. We simply should not be surprised that our practices will not pay out in equal and corresponding levels of return.

HARD TRUTH #6:

PAY WHAT'S FAIR, PAY WHAT'S COMPETITIVE, AND PAY WHAT'S RIGHT, BUT DON'T EXPECT EMPLOYEES TO RECOGNIZE IT, OR BE APPRECIATIVE OR LOYAL BECAUSE OF IT.

INTENTIONALITY

Intentional speech and actions mean clarity of mind and purpose

———

"I said intention." A down-and-out Cecil Rhodes was seeking to borrow a large sum of money from the wealthiest wool broker in London.

"Pardon, so you did. I thought it was an unheedful use of the word—an unheedful valuing of its strength you know."

"I knew its strength."

"Well I must say—but look here..."

Cecil Rhodes continued, "I shall make 200,000 pounds out of it in 60 days."

"You mean, of course, that you might make it if..."

"I said, shall."

"Yes, by George, you did say shall! You are the most definite devil I ever saw in the matter of language. Dear, dear, dear, look here! Definite speech means clarity of mind."

—*from* Cecil Rhodes and the Shark *(1893) by Mark Twain*

Hopefully, readers are solid in their Twain and know that Rhodes borrowed the money and indeed secured a fortune for himself and the wool broker. Hopefully too, the lesson on definite speech resonated.

Intentionality is the practice of saying intentional things, doing intentional things, and living intentional lives. The alternative is that we are merely flotsam, washed around by the current and prevailing tides.

Living a life of intentionality should be common and commonplace. Managers and leaders should make intentional decisions, workers should do intentional work, banks should intentionally protect my money, people should intentionally drive their automobiles, and parents should intentionally raise their children. If it were but so easy…

Intentionality begins with a joust between habits and decisions. And, like most of human life and actions, our decisions are directed by our language just as we talk our way through rationalizing our habits. This happens through the words we use and, of course, the actions we then take. Sometimes, an observer cannot readily see the difference between a habitual life and an intentional one. But over time, habits are exposed and intent unveiled. "Where did I put my keys?" "Have you seen my phone?" "I just did it out of habit." These questions and phrases tend to show a life of randomness and ingrained habit. It seems silly to suggest that one not managing her or his keys has carryover into business performance, but it does.

For certain, the military believes it does. From early on in my infantry officer training, seemingly absurd relationships were made. "If you cannot make your bunk properly, how can we trust you to call in artillery or air strikes to support your mission?" Intellectually, of course, we knew there was no relationship between bunks and air strikes, but we learned that habits are excuses and leaders make intentional choices. This is a book on leadership, not on habit-driven lives.

HABITS ARE EXCUSES; LEADERS MAKE INTENTIONAL CHOICES.

So it is in life and business. Choices daily. My son and I used to joke about whether "today" was the day we started smoking. Of course we didn't (and don't), but we were reinforcing that it was a choice—to start, or stop—and that each day we would make an intentional decision that we would live with. For that day. A decision, not a habit. We talked about it intentionally, because language is powerful; your language and the choices you make define you.

In the western movie *True Grit*, Marshal Rooster Cogburn, played by John Wayne in the first film (1969) and Jeff Bridges in the remake (2010), is questioned in court about a shoot-out that resulted in several wanted outlaws dead. Cogburn explains that he was "backing away" from one man as they began to draw their guns and fire.

"And Marshal Cogburn, what direction were you going at this time?"

"Backwards," he replied. "I always go backwards when I am backing up." Rooster Cogburn spoke intentionally and purposefully.

Intentionality can be challenging for leaders. So many people go through life on autopilot, allowing events to define them and their work, and accepting habits as choices. They struggle to communicate with intentional messages and intentional leaders. In fact, they often do not believe that you mean what you say. It begins with the little things. If you schedule a meeting to begin at 8 a.m., then begin at 8 a.m. It shows respect for those in attendance, gives a message to those who are late, and establishes that you intend to follow what you have said and what you have scheduled. You don't need to punish those who are late or lock them out; over time, they eventually will correct their behavior (a good result) or self-select out of your organization (an equally good result).

Obviously, one meeting or one intentional comment or act does not establish a practice of intentionality. It comes from your choice to be intentional in your life. Do you wear your seat belt every time you are in the car? Do you do it from habit or do you wear it with intention each time? That is the difference. Do you dress intentionally for meetings or events? Do you exercise intentionally or just slog through junk minutes on the machine?

I recently saw *Sully*, the Tom Hanks movie about the US Airways plane piloted by Captain Chesley Sullenberger. In the 208 seconds fate gave him to make decisions and save his passengers and crew (or not), Captain Sullenberger did nothing out of habit. He made intentional choices based upon his training and his judgment, and safely landed on the Hudson River.

As the subsequent investigations wore on, he made it clear that it was an intentional water landing—not a crash landing—and that his plane was "on" the Hudson, not "in" the Hudson when they evacuated passengers and crew. Exactly. Intentional statements from an intentional man doing intentional work.

In Hard Truth #4, I portrayed a sample conversation preparing a team leader to go back to her team and improve an aspect of their work. As I said there, when you mentor staff, you don't just make it up. You choose each word that you teach them to say. You empower them with language and belief and give them a strategy you believe will work. That is your job. To have a playbook, to know your playbook, and to use your playbook. Leaders lead and mentor by intent.

Ask yourself how many of the approximately 65 (or more) offensive plays per game for each team in the National Football League are sent in by the coach with no strategy behind them. The answer, of course, is zero. Every play is expected to accomplish something consistent with the coach's belief system. So it should be in management. Do not do useless things. (See Hard Truth #5). Have a belief system, have a plan and playbook, and "run it" over and over with precise intentionality. And, of course, live your life in a similar fashion. Your employees will note if you are not what you say or what you wish them to be.

"If you say you will do a thing, you must do exactly that thing," said the Colombian drug lord to undercover cops Sonny Crockett and Ricardo Tubbs (*Miami Vice*, 2006). Let's agree that there are typically more negative consequences for not following through with promises to a drug lord. No merit raise... and no knee caps. But organizational work and leadership is too often overly sloppy. Missed communications, questioned missions and visions, lack of focus, and lost clients—not to mention lost client loyalty and revenue—often come without consequences. We can be better, but only if we intend to be so.

Be careful, though, intentionality can appear to have a tone. People will ask you the same questions over and over, and ask them differently each time. They will expect different answers on sliding sound bite scales. They will be frustrated and sometimes unappreciative when you answer them the same way, each and every time, with precision. With no variance. I recall conversations about a building project I was in charge of. I inherited it late and it was behind schedule. When asked, I repeatedly stated, "We will finish it on time and within budget." What followed was like a comedy—just not very funny.

"But you can't mean on time with the original schedule?"

"Yes, we'll complete it on time."

"But that's not realistic since much of the building fund is already spent."

"The building fund is fine; we will be within our budget."

"But you don't mean the original budget; won't you have to go back to the taxpayers for more money?"

"No, I mean we'll finish it on time and within budget."

"But surely that doesn't mean…"

We did finish it on time, and actually under budget. Not because I am a miracle worker; it was simply the result of good people working hard on a project they were committed to. And I didn't care that it frustrated people when I gave the same (correct) answer over and over. For some reason, people are not used to intentional language. They try to drive wedges between what you want to say and what you say. Precision of language and intentionality of thought, word, and action will be your friend.

Intentionality can also be confused with arrogance, an accusation tossed at me regarding the building project recounted above, and over my career. For me, it is simply my knowledge and confidence of intentionality. I am no better than any other person, but I strive to live an intentional life, do intentional things, and say intentional things for intentional purposes. I work to have no habits, but rather make (intentional) decisions about each thing I do. When people get to know me, they understand.

I simply do not know how we could allow ourselves to waste our precious and fleeting lives and opportunities to lead and make a difference through unintentional behavior. We are better than flotsam.

HARD TRUTH #7:

LEADERSHIP IS NOT YOUR COLLECTION OF HABITS, IT IS FORGED AND DEFINED BY YOUR INTENTIONALITY.

HARD TRUTH #8

LEADERSHIP

The situation always rules

———

"Where are the workers?" I asked.

"We pulled them off the job and sent them to another one in Seattle," the construction manager replied. It was my first day on the job. I had agreed to help a very small and very rural school district get its new school built. The superintendent had quit in a huff and the planned $12,000,000 school was not getting built. Now it was up to me.

"Why did you do that, pull your workers off the job?" I asked.

"Because you are suing us and we are not going to build another inch of your school while you're suing."

In short, I had signed on to a mess. It was fall and sleeting. The school's foundation was poured with a few pieces of steel jutting upward, but nothing more. I had just been hired as the school district superintendent, and now had just found out that we were suing our construction company. Great!

"Get them back," I said to the construction manager.

"What?"

"Get them back. I want the school built, so get the workers back."

"But what about the lawsuit?" he asked.

"We're not suing anyone," I replied. "You and I will meet every week. You'll let me know of every problem or needed change. Now, let's build the school."

He stared at me and slowly asked, "You are dropping the lawsuit?" I looked back at him and said nothing. After a moment he nodded, turned, and got on his phone.

The next day we had five workers, and the day after that, 20. We built the school on time and under budget. It opened the next fall to the delight of the children, the teachers, and the community.

Of all people, I am not a construction person, not even a home handyman, but I knew that this was a people problem—it was leadership they needed from me, not hanging steel. I was there, asked by a friend who ran the superintendent vacancy search to help the district, and then its board. They had waited years to pass a bond for a new school, and now it was in peril. It was not a situation I fancied myself in, but the situation rules—it always gets its way. The messier it is, the more leadership it takes. And it's the mess leaders need to like.

This is a book on leadership, yet only one chapter title bears the word. Truthfully, all 19 chapters are about leadership, but this one gets to the heart and psyche of leaders. You either love the work or you do not.

Time and again, I have had friends and colleagues complain to me about their jobs. "I love the job, but I just hate the politics."

"Then why did you take a political job?" I would ask.

"I didn't," was invariably the reply. But, of course, they did.

"I love my work, but I hate the constant hammering from corporate about the budget. It wears me out."

"Then why did you take a finance job?"

"I didn't." They did.

The problem with many managers and "leaders" is that they do love the cosmetics of the job. They love many of the people, their product or service, clients, the day-to-day work, the location, maybe the prestige, and even the salary. But that one nagging thing that their bosses won't let up on, the thing that keeps higher-ups up at night worrying, is the thing they should most embrace. That is what they are paid to fix. For whatever you are paid to fix, you should also love fixing it.

I often wonder why bright people with college degrees in management seem surprised that office politics, budget, new client acquisition, sales growth, production deadlines, and one metric after another are part of the job. Why are we surprised that the more we are paid, the less "clean" the work? The less clear. The less easily defined and step-by-step. In other words, the more it requires *leadership,* and not just do-the-next-step management.

Imagine professional football players hating to play outdoors in the elements. Or race car drivers complaining about others zipping around them so fast. "I love driving the race car, but this constant emphasis on speed and winning is getting to me." Then you're not a race car driver.

So it is with leadership.

WHEN YOU WRESTLE A PIG YOU BOTH GET MUDDY, BUT THE PIG LOVES IT.

Welcome to pigdom—and the mess that comes with it—if you want to be a leader. McKinsey star, best-selling author, and management guru Tom Peters wrote "50 Rules for Leaders," (*Fast Company*, March 2001), and Rule #3 was "Leaders Love the Mess." While my military training had me versed on orderly leadership, my first civilian management boss, circa 1981, prepped me for what Peters would ultimately write 20 years later. I had a problem in my department and I approached him with, "Bob, I've got a huge problem."

He replied, "No young man, you have an opportunity to excel." And so it was. And so I learned that the mess is why we are hired, and why we make the proverbial "big bucks."

Big bucks notwithstanding, nor forthcoming, as incoming chair of a small state university's school of business, I had a mess. This time, though, I knew it coming in, and was hired to fix things. I had assured the university president that I could do this. I am a social scientist. This is what I do; I'm an organizational development guy, not an accountant.

A dozen faculty greeted me. Good professors with strong egos, and most with a story of how they had been treated badly by the previous chair or by colleagues up and down the hall. So be it. At our first meeting I laid out how I worked—with intentionality; how I communicated—authentically; what I expected from them—do your job. I didn't care about last year. I couldn't change or fix last year. We were moving forward. They, of course, wanted to talk about last year.

After several attempts to redirect them to this year, I simply stood up and told them they could talk about last year as much as they wished, but would do it without me. When they were ready to move forward, they should let me know. I walked out. About 30 minutes later, my administrative assistant called me and said, "Dr. Tomlin, I think the faculty are ready to move forward." And so they were. Some faculty leaders had taken control of the meeting, and they were ready.

That this had been a mess didn't bother me, but some of them apologized to me for almost a year. We laughed about it, developed a good team, and did some excellent work over the next few years. I learned that many of them simply did not believe nor trust me at the beginning. They had heard it before, in their business and corporate experiences and then in higher education.

Over time, one by one, they came to my office with a problem that needed fixing, apologizing for bringing it to me. Whatever have we done, in management and in leadership, that people feel it necessary to apologize for bringing issues, or problems, or mistakes, or messes to us? We get the big office for a reason. We know it is our job to advance our organization's strategic positions, so why do we sometimes decry the work that does that? We need to love it. Every day.

Fixing the mess is what we are paid to do. Preventing it is better, but messes happen. Knowing that you are there to solve it, to fix it, to prevent your bosses from staying awake at night worrying, is not just leadership—it is the fun part. Welcome to pigdom...have you ever seen pigs not having fun?

Yet messes don't stay cleaned up. And yes, my successors inherited one of their own. That is the nature of leadership. Hopefully they love it every day.

HARD TRUTH #8:

LOVE THE WORK AND THE ACCOMPANYING MESS— OR LEAVE IT.

HARD TRUTH #9
FOCUS
You can multitask, but few can multi-focus

I recently participated in an online discussion on the topic of whether men or women were better at multitasking. The participants were largely upper-level managers with a few business school faculty, like myself, tossed in. Women edged men as the better multitaskers pretty easily, and the reason cited was their experience managing children, the household, and work.

While that may sound sexist to some, it is hard to deny women their place in these traditional roles, even as they are at least—for the last generation—newly traditioned into upper management, and at the highest levels. Yet, the most surprising pattern in the debate was the constant complaints about multitasking itself. Comment after comment came from executives decrying the lack of focus in the workplace, sometimes from the most important or impactful players. They do too many things at the same time and get too few things done right, on time, and on schedule.

The hard truth is that, for most mortals, so-called multitasking is simply a bunch of hooey, an excuse for not paying attention to details, or for a lack of ability to focus on what is important at a given time. An excuse for wandering through an unintentional day.

Yet, it is a fair argument that, in today's nanosecond world, we need new focusing skills, the ability to sift and sort, and to input nonstop data without losing our focus on whatever is important at the time. A question by a 57-year-old woman to Dr. Mehmet Oz, host of the *Dr. Oz* television show, voiced a concern over smartphone distractions and whether it was a sign of future cognitive problems. Dr. Oz responded that "Humans crave distraction." He went on to give tips about focusing our lives in a cell phone world, with ideas such as not turning on our phones unless we are checking them for calls or messages.

It should be devastating to us that, as an intelligent and evolved species, we must be told to set aside distractions in order to focus—whether focusing on work, driving, walking, or making sure we don't forget our children and leave them in a hot car.

Dr. Oz went on to discuss how a lack of self-esteem causes us to crave the attention our distractions bring. Every distraction makes us feel important to someone or something. Of course, we can simply ween ourselves off the distraction dependency by improving our self-esteem and self-respect, and learning to "focus" on leading intentional lives and doing intentional work.

The need for distraction importance very likely explains the young cell phone culture of nonstop attention to the device. Studies of college students have shown they are pretty poor multitaskers. In "Faculty Focus," (9/12/2012, Magna Publications) five different research studies are shown with hundreds of college students as participants, resulting in the conclusion that only about 5 percent can multitask effectively. So how do we get them to focus? It takes leadership and attention.

*"A wealth of information creates a poverty of
attention."*

—Herbert Simon, noted economist, 1971

Best-selling author and psychologist Daniel Goleman writes in the *Harvard Business Review* (December 2013) that "A primary task of leadership is to direct attention." This is the very attention that is referenced in Herbert Simon's quote above. Goleman goes on to discuss the neuroscience of attention and distraction, and makes the case that "focus" is more than simply filtering out distractions; you also must *be* focused. And Goleman believes that leadership emanates from those who can focus on others and direct their attention.

For leaders to bring their A game, they must filter and gain the attention of their subordinates to purposefully engage the work. We need all of our other managers, staff, and line employees to be good at their work and to be solely engaged with it. We need them to be focused and intentional. We may not readily solve financial poverty, but as leaders, if we can solve Simon's "poverty of attention," that would be a huge breakthrough in productivity.

Professional golf is certainly intentional work, and Simon's "wealth of information" was surely what golfer Tiger Woods faced on the final hole needed to win one of his many major tournament victories. He was 200 yards out, the green was two levels, with trees tight to the rear, three sand traps guarding the front, and slope leading to water on the right. He put the ball a few feet from the hole and sank his putt for the victory. Shortly afterward, he was interviewed and asked how he could so coolly focus and not be distracted by all of those hazards. "What hazards?" Tiger asked. "I was looking at the pin; I guess I never saw those other things." He went on to explain that since he never intended to hit his ball into the trees, sand, or water, he paid no attention to them. He was hitting to the pin, he was looking at the pin, and he was focused on the pin with the same exact kind of laser focus the Google development team had in their 130-hour workweeks.

"No, no, no, I can tell that you are looking for mistakes." The sergeant first class sounded frustrated, but he really was being patient. "If you look for what is right and what is wrong at the same time, you will see neither." Sounding more like kung fu or Confucius than the U.S. Army, my instructor at Jumpmaster School was teaching me a lesson about focus. Learn to look for perfect parachutes. Focus only on what perfection looks like, and disregard the rest.

I was a young Army captain and an experienced parachutist, but now I was learning the intricate details of inspecting both parachutes and soldiers prior to jumping out of airplanes. The rule just sounded too simple: Learn what perfect parachutes look like, and look for perfect parachutes. We had been taught for days about how parachutes were to be rigged and what they should look like, a.k.a. "perfect parachutes," but it seemed logical that we would also learn about problems or mistakes in rigging so we could quickly spot them. That was a loser's game, I would learn. If you think you know what mistakes to look for, you'll miss the mistake(s) you didn't know about. So, you don't look for them. You look for perfect parachutes, and any deviation from that bears very close inspection.

Perfect parachutes. Once you have that indelibly etched in your mind, you can truly focus. Know what customer service should look like and focus on getting it right, not trying to fix problems. Know what your production floor should look like, and focus on that—getting it right. Have a vision of your work done perfectly, and keep that as your focus. A true focus. Not some multitasky-focus hocus-pocus that seems millennially convenient and stylish. But rather, a true focus on work, on project after project, one thing done, done perfectly and precisely, and then moving to the next with intentionality.

HARD TRUTH #9:

LEADERS FOCUS ON MISSION, PEOPLE, AND OUTCOMES, AND DISREGARD THE NOISE.

GRIT

Courage can misfire, while grit continues to reload

———

"**M**ister, you've sure got a lot of hard bark on you." It was actor Richard Boone talking to Paul Newman (*Hombre*, 1967). Hard bark. I never forgot those words, although the movie is forgettable with Newman terribly miscast as a half-breed Indian. Boone is never miscast. But *Hombre* was a pleasure of stereotypical, tough-guy language and occasional western action.

Today hard bark is making a comeback. Not as a phrase, but rather as an idea and maybe a movement. Psychologist Angela Duckworth's *New York Times* best-selling *Grit: The Power of Passion and Perseverance* (Scribner, 2016) is the book I would have written if I had been both me and Angela Duckworth… It is the perfect book about doing hard things, and the perfect book to relaunch grit into our lexicon—and maybe our national and personal character.

The United States is a nation gone soft. Our college students demanding to be coddled and protected from challenging ideas and language; one anti-bullying workshop and program after another in our public schools; workers demanding to be protected from the free market that creates their jobs. The list is endless. True grit? More like no grit. Our hard bark has been soaked off by a culture of victimhood and entitlements.

It seems like forever, but, in relation to the world, it was not that long ago that a young and vibrant (U.S.) President John F. Kennedy nailed the grit of America, twice—first in his inaugural address (1961) "...*ask not what your country can do for you, ask what you can do for your country.*" A plea to the grit of a people still building a nation, just over 15 years since the end of World War II. A people who Kennedy knew put country first, and had both the courage and the grit to keep it there.

He spoke again of our grit in 1962, about his goals of space exploration and putting a man on the moon then returning him safely home. His words "...*we do these things not because they are easy but because they are hard...*" exemplified the hard bark on the American people. Yes, we do it precisely because it is hard. We are Americans, after all.

That was then. Now is now. Now, a time when the hardest issue government seems to want to deal with is which toilet we should be directed to use. But we learned in physics that for every action, there is an equal and opposite reaction. And sometimes, laws of the hard sciences find themselves in the social sciences. So maybe the pendulum is swinging, and maybe we still have a modicum of that grit. Maybe it has not all been lost to stylish millennialism. For sure, Angela Duckworth came out swinging, comparatively studying survivors of West Point and those who dropped out, the survivors of Army Special Forces (Green Berets) training and those who dropped out, and many more. It doesn't get much grittier, although she began crafting her theories as a seventh-grade math teacher in New York.

Yet Duckworth's book is actually the second major contemporary clarion call to self-action. Facebook COO Sheryl Sandberg started the current party with *Lean In: Women, Work and the Will to Lead* (Borzoi-Knopf, 2013) and founded her *LeanIn. Org* site along with Lean In Circles for women leaders to seek networking, skills, and training. The two-penny difference is that Sandberg writes to help women leaders, and Duckworth writes about life attitudes and skills for all.

For us as leaders, the hard truth is that leadership *is* about life. You can't lead if you are not a leader. You can't model behavior to your employees if you are not a model. And if you can't "stay the course," other personal attributes and factors will not achieve success for you. This is a message America should not need. We are the land of opportunity, not the land of guarantees. But it is the concept of guarantees we have drifted toward.

In Asia, I saw the very poor, without their own land, farming rice in the backwater of a river and living under a large bridge. An unexpected heavy rain would flood the river and wash their mud dams away, but you would see them the very next day fashioning their dams and replanting what they could. Grit. They were a lesson and an inspiration to me. No guarantees, just their indefatigable perseverance. Work, feed your family, expect nothing from others, survive. Grit.

COURAGE STANDS TALL TODAY. GRIT IS UNYIELDING OVER TIME.

And therein lies the difference between courage and grit. Courage is an act or action while grit is a continuation, a perseverance of effort. We could argue that President Barack Obama showed courage by enacting policy by fiat of executive order during his presidency. But in eight years as president, he never displayed the grit to sit with congressional leaders and hammer out the necessary legislation needed to serve our nation better. Similarly, it is fair to point out that neither did our congressional leaders show such grit.

It took courage for Mary Barra to accept the position of CEO of General Motors. A career engineer and manager at GM, Barra is the first woman CEO of any major automobile manufacturer. It has taken grit to deal day in and day out with the flawed ignition switch problem and scandal that rocked GM. It was not her fault or mistake, but it is her mess to clean up. Leaders love the mess (see Hard Truth #8) and Barra has gritted GM to new style and platform lineups, and one industry award after another. Maybe we still have it.

It took courage for American Express CEO Kenneth Chenault to stay at the helm after losing AMEX's largest customer when Costco bolted to VISA. Some thought Costco was too big a loss to overcome, and predicted dire times for the storied and proud AMEX. But Chenault went "Blue" with new cards and programs, and, as of this writing, earnings per share are far exceeding analysts' projections. The courage to stay, the grit to see it through, and the leadership to tackle the mess.

Grit is seldom flashy, and likely will not design your next new "it" product or service. But grit sustains. Grit fuels your spizzerinctum. Grit is there for you when all else fails. And it is hard to imagine what we could use more of in our homes, schools, government, and industries.

HARD TRUTH #10:

GRIT MAKES NO EXCUSES AND GETS IT DONE, OVER AND OVER.

HARD TRUTH #11
POWER
Power accumulates, and leadership rides on its back

———

It was the annual Christmas party for the corporation. Albertsons grocery stores, to be exact, and I was there with my wife. She worked at corporate headquarters in Boise, Idaho. The founder, the late Joe Albertson, was a legend in the town where he started his first store and more so in the corporate offices. A grocery man through and through. The party was fun and the food was great, at least as great as the lines to the cash bar. But Mr. Albertson, while gone, was not forgotten.

Historically, there was a head table at the parties for corporate and board dignitaries and, of course, Joe's place was at the center. Except that he wasn't ever there—the story is legend. He was always, predictably, where he belonged, in the crowd talking with his grocery store managers and produce people and those he most loved—grocery store folk. But then one year, it was time for evening comments, and Joe's staff and handlers were getting nervous. He needed to be at the head table. They sent an emissary to fetch him.

"Mr. Albertson, excuse me, but you are needed at the head table," the young man said. "Son, wherever I sit is the head table," was Mr. Albertson's polite yet very direct reply. Powerful people aren't fetched. Shortly after, but in his own time, he got up and joined the dignitaries to make comments and continue the Christmas festivities on into the night. Each year at the Christmas party, Albertson old-timers reveled in telling that story.

"…Wherever I sit is the head table." His words were geographically false, but undeniably true. As the story was told to me, I could almost hear him speak. But I do recognize the simple, polite, and absolute power that he had exerted. Power, not leadership. That was for day-in and day-out work with the corporation. This was power, and he had just invested a small portion of his to make a statement.

Leadership studies and too many books give short shrift to power. We should eschew power, we are told, and endeavor to be better leaders. If we are using power to lead, it must be because we are failing at leadership. What a bunch of malarkey. First and foremost, leadership is a social science, not a hard science. And decades ago, Nobel laureate Bertrand Russell stated that "the fundamental concept in social science is Power…" Young children don't respond to their parents' leadership; they respond to their parents' power to give or take away, to make happen or to prevent or deny. Similarly, the 1960s-era Soviet Union did not respond to (U.S.) President Kennedy's leadership during the Cuban Missile Crisis, but they did respond to his naval blockade. Kennedy's threats were just a bad check waiting to be called out, without the power of the U.S. Navy to back it.

The hard truth is that power is every bit as essential to your success as leadership. We are disadvantaged in the English-speaking world because our language does not allow us to treat power with equal respect to leadership. Consider these three words: lead, leader, and leadership. Now, what are their power equivalents in the oft-wanting English language?

- Lead is to "power" as (*"She needs to power her way through this."*)

- Leader is to "powerer" as (*"He is our best powerer."*)

- Leadership is to "powership" as (*"It was a brilliant display of powership."*)

My spellcheck doesn't like the usage, and yours likely doesn't either. But let's agree that there are those in "leadership" positions who would qualify more as "powerers," if the word existed. The word may not exist, but the concept does. For all of us.

It is not just those who cannot lead and use power as a crutch or a club who dance at power's door. It is also those who *can* lead and who understand very well the role of leadership, who use power as an important currency to get things done and keep their seat warm in the next higher position. Power used well is power used with intentionality (see Hard Truth #7).

Asking how one obtains power is like asking how Mark Zuckerberg obtained his money. For Zuckerberg, founder and CEO of Facebook, his money came in two ways: 1) He created it out of the air through an invention, and 2) he got it from us. So it is with power. Some power we accumulate over time with our natural work and position. It comes with the air. Other power we gain by replacing people, or striking deals for which others then owe us, or by winning victories that exalt us and/ or diminish others.

Much of Zuckerberg's power is in a latent form, just sitting in the bank, and that often is power enough, like the law enforcement officer's sidearm on her belt—it need not always be drawn to support the badge.

I know that I have failed twice in my career to use power to my advantage and to that of my organization. Both times we settled for mediocrity, when I know today I could have been a more effective "powerer" and settled for more, not less. Both times I overrelied on my strong suit, people skills, and let the power I had accumulated lie fallow. It is, of course, clearer to me today…

POWER NOT OCCASIONALLY SPENT IS NOT POWER AT ALL.

Robert Greene, author of the most excellent book *The 48 Laws of Power* (Penguin, 1998) writes that to effectively use power, we must accept it as a "game." You "play" with a strategy and continually observe your opponent, much as a master card player might across the table. As a social scientist, I understand and enjoy that part. But power won't wait, and it doesn't choose winners. Greene went on to say "do not commit to anyone." Once you commit support to someone, they "possess" you—and you lose all power with and over them. Losing power was the part I misplayed. I relied on loyalty and commitment in return, overestimating both.

In positions of leadership, we are granted legitimate power (see French & Raven's Bases of Power, 1959) for our position, and presumably informational power or expert power (op cit) for the content knowledge of our work. But none of those have transactional power—the power needed to truly effect change in an organization, to repurpose, to change our practices or focus.

"When you meet a swordsman, draw your sword."

—From a Ch'an Buddhist classic,
translated by Thomas Cleary, 1993

If leaders are to make hard and contested decisions, they must have a sword in their hand, and that sword will be the two-edged blade of coercive and reward power (op cit). Reward and punishment—pleasure and pain. Ultimately, human decisions come back to the base emotional and psychological motivators we have known about since our first introduction to psychology class in undergraduate school.

The application and expenditure of power at the proper time will soften the opposition for your leadership strategy to run through. As there are times in world affairs for a diplomat and times for a navy, so it is in organizational leadership. Protect your brand and image (see Hard Truth #18), keep commitments to a minimum of the most loyal, and use the sword of power strategically and sufficiently so that it does not diminish and is never doubted.

HARD TRUTH #11:

POWER BUYS YOU THE MOST WHEN YOU SPEND IT REGULARLY.

STRATEGY

If you don't have a theory you won't have a strategy

———

I was new to the firm, an upper-middle manager, and the CEO knew I was experienced in strategic planning. The board was ready for a new five-year plan, so the CEO asked me to facilitate the process. They had a plan, many pages developed by a high-priced professional facilitator, and the CEO gave it to me. We set a meeting with the executive team a few weeks ahead.

As I read through the plan and began to prep, I quickly saw we were in trouble. I discovered the "plan" was 15 pages of stand-alone "strategies," followed by a 16-page "Task Addendum." It was no plan at all. A lot of people had participated in a lot of work developing pages and pages of near-useless lists of things. It was maybe, at best, a task directive and calendar, but it was in no way *strategic*.

I read and reread the strategies: "remodel facilities" and "provide professional development for employees," along with "ensure fiscal discipline." And pages more. "Maintain our bond rating." *Cool*, I thought, *that will propel us beyond our competitors. They will never think of these things.* My thoughts were snarky, and snarky would not play with the boss nor help me. I had to see him.

But then I began to doubt. I was in a bit of a fix. If this was what they were wanting, simply renewed, I was not their guy. Yet it was handed to me by the CEO. I decided to go ahead and prep for the first meeting, so in advance I compiled and distributed a few articles and guidelines on strategic planning, and a brief agenda for our meeting via email. I heard nothing back.

At the meeting, it became clear that they indeed wanted to just update the list of things. I shocked them a little by asking what they considered to be the "theory" of the organization. They didn't know what I meant. "You know," I explained, "are we the most innovative, or the cheapest, or the best with customer service? What is our theory—are we a run-first or pass-first football team?"

They assured me the team wanted to be all those things, so, of course, we were none. The strategic planning effort faltered and, after a few sessions, the CEO let it drift to the side. As it turned out, we lost clients and our bond rating was downgraded over the next few years. Eventually, I left the organization.

Knowing, understanding, or selecting the theory of your organization is a critical preliminary step to determining the strategies you will employ. Todd Zinger, writing in the *Harvard Business Review* (June 2013), explains the secret sauce of the Walt Disney Company: "...*comic strips promote films; films feed material to comic strips;...Disneyland plugs movies, and movies plug the park.*" He went on to explain that the Disney Channel publicizes Disney's "products of the music division," while the film division feeds "tunes and talent" to the music division.

Disney was theorized and created as a perfect value-creating, self-synergized entity even before the technology was available that would advance it to today's heights. Theory first, then strategy. With theory in hand, Disney could follow the strategic steps of defining where they wished to compete, how they intended to win, and how they were going to move from advantage to advantage.*

> *"Focus on your one purpose."*
>
> —Japanese motto

While seemingly very diverse in entertainment, Disney could easily be said to have but one focus—create value in entertainment. That would be the theory undergirding all of the surface activities and strategies.

So it is with any organization: theory first and strategy second. But what of strategy? Didn't my former organization have a strategic plan and pages of strategies? Sort of. The point of strategy is that it must *be* strategic, and that's what my firm didn't have and seemed to avoid. A list of activities or goals is seldom strategic.

"Remodeling facilities," as mentioned above, is not strategic, *unless* we are getting beat by competitors due to their better facilities, or unless we are losing customers and clients due to outmoded facilities. Then the remodel is not about remodeling; it is about customer or client acquisition and retention, service and satisfaction. We must know the theory behind our facilities. What is it we expect them to do for us, beyond letting us work inside, protected from the weather?

Think of a new CEO coming into an aging company. Does he immediately spend money on upgrading the e-suite to show that class and modernization have now arrived and will soon follow throughout? Does she not spend a dime on her office digs and instead shove money into research and development, or manufacturing upgrades, or marketing and advertising? A good executive will make those decisions with a plan, with intentionality (see Hard Truth #7), with a theory behind them on what the actions should cause to happen, and with a strategy unfolding on how that theory borne into action will improve the organization's strategic position.

Strategy, to be effective, does not require a plan. Strategy requires a belief system and the courage and skill to run your belief system "strategically," over and over, to push your theory forward. A strategic plan is nice, but if it does not outline *strategy*, then it is too often just a pack of to-do tasks all stapled together.

There are two basic strategy questions to ask as you grapple with this idea of strategy.

1. Is this "strategy" something that all firms and organizations do, including your competitors? If so, what is strategic about how you do it? Can you do it faster, better, cheaper? Put that in your plan.

2. (Or) Is this "strategy" something that is rare to you, or distinctive to you and your organization? And if so—so what? Will it help you win? Will it gain customers and clients? Will it increase revenue? If so, put that in your plan.

Ultimately, your theories and strategies, as you put them into play, begin to define and operationalize your mission (see Hard Truth #4), and support and expose the vision you have for the future of your organization. And, since most modern organizations want a "strategic plan," you should probably have one too. But make certain that it meets the criteria of its name. Make certain that it is strategic, and that it is a plan.

HARD TRUTH #12:

A STRATEGIC PLAN IS NOT A STRATEGY. GET ONE (A STRATEGY) OR FALL BEHIND.

*Steps credited to Rita Gunther McGrath, *The End of Competitive Advantage,* (HBR Press, 2013). Gunther is a professor at Columbia Business School.

HARD TRUTH #13

SELF

Get yourself together, then your company

The young boy was constantly bothering his dad, who was trying to watch a football game on television. Finally, the man picked up a magazine, thumbed through it and found a full-page map of the world, and tore out the page. He got up and found some scissors, then cut the page into small pieces. Handing the mess of pieces to his son, he said, "Here's a puzzle, let's see how fast you can put it together." Back to football and some quiet.

The boy quickly put the puzzle together with tape and summoned his father. "How did you put this together so fast?" his dad asked.

"It was easy. On the other side of the map was a picture of a man. Once I got the man together right, the world was right, too."

And so it is. When we are put together right, our companies can be put together right, too. Or our cities, state, or nation. But only then.

Taking care of ourselves is not narcissistic. What are we taught to do in airplanes if we experience a "sudden loss of cabin pressure"? Place our oxygen mask securely on before we help others. The point is that we likely have others to help, and cannot do so if we are struggling.

What are we paid for in our work? To improve our organization's strategic position by whatever metrics we are judged. In order to be most effective with our work, we must be at our most effective selves. The hard truth is that *we* are the biggest challenge to our management. We understand when employees have "life," illness, or attitude interrupt critical work cycles, but ourselves? That is a different issue, and can be a battle.

We are mortal, but the rule of life is that it is a "do-it-to-yourself" program. We have total control over much of it, some control over most of it, and no control over only very small parts of it. The key to managing the self well is to manage perfectly that which we can control, and to not worry about the rest.

MASTER YOUR LIFE TO MASTER YOUR WORK.

Mastering your life seems too simple and, at the same time, too impossible a task. A catchy phrase, but really? Yes, really. If we lead intentional lives (see Hard Truth #7) we likely are already in control of our life and self. And truly, if we cannot manage our self, why should we be trusted with a company?

IBM fully understood this during their glory days. The days when their personal computers were the gold standard and they had simply the best and most powerful advertising slogan in the computer wars: *"Nobody ever got fired for buying IBM."* At the same time, IBM had a very quirky executive interview technique. Fly a couple of executives to the hometown of the interviewee and direct him (they were mainly men, then) to pick them up at the airport. The traveling execs would invariably have luggage and bags, and need to stow them in the trunk of the car. Inspection time…if the trunk was clean, that was good, but if it was a mess—beer cans, fish bait, diapers, or otherwise filthy—then it was clear the interviewee was not IBM material. If you cannot manage your trunk, how will you manage an organization?

So, how do you manage yourself? It is with your actions. You begin, right after cleaning your car's trunk, by committing to maintaining control of your language, your temper, and your actions, and resolve to model the behavior that just might be IBM material. Your team and coworkers can see you emotional, but they should not see you as irrational or out of control.

Second, leaders move on. Our self often wants to dwell in the past, live our failures, hold grudges, seek revenge for wrongdoing, or continue to blame events, people, regulations, or coworkers who may have let you down. Leaders give themselves a short getting-over-it period, then move on. Our self will come with us, but we must direct it.

Third, leaders stay happy and optimistic. We learned from Viktor Frankl in *Man's Search for Meaning* (1946) that we cannot control everything that happens to us, but we can control how we respond. Frankl, of course, survived the Jewish death camps of World War II, and is credited with helping many develop the attitude to survive. Most of us can only imagine the horrors and atrocities of those camps, but we can notice that our lots in life are markedly better. And that is sufficient in and of itself to be happy. Problems at work? We get paid to fix them and, of course, as leaders we love the mess (see Hard Truth #8). Happy is a choice. Optimistic is a choice.

And leaders stay healthy. Managing yourself means taking care of your hard drive and software. I am not the first to note that there are three pillars of self-maintenance: diet, exercise, and sleep. Only three, so how hard can that be? Really. Eat with a plan, mostly, when you can. Schedule exercise time into your 24-hour day and 168-hour week (see Hard Truth #5), and plan for adequate sleep.

Unmanaged selves have 1,000 excuses for why they simply cannot manage those three pillars. They are right. And they are right because they are unmanaged selves. A trunk full of garbage that needs someone to take control. A life in pieces like the cut-up paper the father gave his son. Yet, when the boy realized there was a person on one side, he was able to take control and put the person together; thus, the world was put together.

Such is our opportunity as leaders. Take control of our self, and we will far better manage the people and the responsibilities entrusted to us.

HARD TRUTH #13:

YOU ARE A "MACROCOSM" OF YOUR TEAM AND YOUR ORGANIZATION, AND YOU MUST MANAGE YOU WELL BEFORE YOU CAN MANAGE THEM AT ALL.

HARD TRUTH #14

DELEGATION

Delegation is strategy, not just job assignment

————

"Larry, who do you think I should delegate this project to? I can't do everything, and I'm going to have to toss this to one of my team."

"Who do you trust enough to not get you fired?" my friend and coworker asked. It's a hard truth that you can delegate the authority to do something to someone else, but you never break free of the responsibility.

Whatever you delegate is your responsibility, being met by other people. It's more than scary, and underscores the importance of your day-to-day leadership. You teach, train, model, and inspire; when the time comes, hopefully your employees will step up and represent you well. Hopefully, because it is *your* job and career on the line.

But this time I didn't delegate. It was too important, and my friend's friendly reminder scared me just enough that I kept this one for myself. I simply moved from 50-hour workweeks to 70 hours. In three tough weeks I finished the project and was nicely recognized for it. But on my annual review, there was a comment that I was "too controlling," meaning better leadership on my part would grow and develop the members of my team so they could do more. Point taken. Fair and accurate.

But even as a young manager, I knew who could do the project best and fastest, and that was me. I also trusted me the most with my career to get it done. I still do. But I know today that such an attitude is simply not sustainable. We pay good people to do work, and it is our fault if they are not contributing at increasingly higher levels. Enter delegation.

There are five basic reasons for delegating work to any particular employee. And to "particular" employees is the only way to delegate. Each act of delegating must be based upon strategy, something you are doing with intentionality (see Hard Truth #7); or else don't delegate at all. Just let the world and your firm run itself by chance and luck. Good luck with that!

BUSINESS IS NOT LITTLE LEAGUE. YOU DO NOT DELEGATE TO THE NEXT PERSON IN LINE BECAUSE IT IS THEIR TURN.

Some employees will think it is their turn to take the lead on a project, and some will think it is their turn to get a pass. Neither is a reason to delegate. It is certainly fair, though, if you have several "lead" quality or lead-experienced employees and you rotate them over time. But that is strategy, and not a default to the "whose turn it is" game.

It is the simple (not hard) truth that your business is in business to make a profit. Your job and that of your employees is to continually advance your company's strategic positions in sales, or market share, or revenue, or client/customer acquisition and retention, or whatever metrics you chase. Every decision you, as a leader, make should be tied to that end. So it is with delegation.

When a significant project comes your way, and you must or want to delegate it to a team member or subordinate, you very likely know immediately who you want to give it to. Of course you do. You're a leader and you have good instincts, so your judgment immediately identifies who should take the lead on that project. But that cannot be the end of your thinking and judgment. Those instincts may continually lead you to the same person, or to yourself. We must grow beyond that.

Our **first** consideration, then, for strategic delegation is: Who will get it done right and on schedule? This generally comes back to your original instincts. You know it immediately; this is your best man or woman who you already rely on. The question now is whether you over-rely on them. Are you taking them from other critical projects? And very importantly, are they the only one to trust with this task? If not you, and not them, then who?

The "who" is your **second** consideration. Which employee "can" do the job and will grow the most from it, and from the responsibility you are handing them? In sports, we think of playing time—minutes in basketball, or "snaps" in football. We ease our young players into the game *if* they have shown the potential. So we do also with rising employees. But, while we can delegate to them, that doesn't end our role or responsibility. We know they are new to this level of work, so we either assign a strong "second chair" or we involve ourselves enough to mentor them, without micromanaging.

Our **third** consideration, which we must make out of respect and with our eye on the reality of office politics and employee retention is: Who is senior and has a "right" to the project and the recognition and rewards that will follow? Depending on your industry, seniority can matter. It matters in many law, engineering, and finance firms. It matters in university life, where faculty rank often reigns. Understand that seniority never makes your decision for you—strategy and judgment do. But we dare not overlook seniority if it matters in our firm. We likely will need to prep the person we are passing over, and/or otherwise incentivize them in order to sustain their loyalty and motivation.

Fourth, we consider who is junior but has earned the right to take the lead, although we may have already addressed this by the time we have worked through our third consideration. We hire our hot "Young Turks" ("young, progressive members of an institution" as defined by *urbandictionary.com*) for a reason. At some point, we need to see what they are made of.

In several early John Wayne cavalry movies, his troop would rescue the women and children but could not outrun the Indians to the safety of the fort. Wayne would invariably need to leave (delegate) a young lieutenant with half of the troop to "hold the river" against the charging Indians while he (Wayne) and the other half of the troop, along with the rescued women and children, hastened to the fort. He always fretted about his decision of whom to leave to face the "hostiles." But make the decision he did, and the young lieutenant would do his duty.* Thank you, West Point. We do the same today with young aspiring managers—it's just that the work, of course, is very different.

The **fifth** and final consideration for delegation is whose turn it is. Though I discounted "turns" as a strategy earlier, it, of course, remains a consideration—just not a very good one in most circumstances. When all things are equal, all employees are equally prepared and qualified, and none of the four previous delegation criteria are valid, then, by all means, use "turns." Most readers and leaders already know that "all things" are never equal.

So, as with John Wayne and the fictional cavalry officers he portrayed, we learn that we can build or destroy a subordinate's career by what we delegate to them *and* by what we withhold. Similarly, our delegation decisions do the same for our careers.

HARD TRUTH #14:

EVERY PROJECT YOU DELEGATE IS YOUR CAREER IN SOMEONE ELSE'S HANDS. DELEGATE IT RIGHT!

*Movie purists will note that the author took the liberty of mixing several John Wayne cavalry movie story lines to make his point.

HARD TRUTH #15

EMPLOYEES

You must never not have enough time for your people

———

The movie was ending, and things were still a mess. Paul Newman may or may not hook up with Sally Field, people were dead but no one was going to prison, and the district attorney was resigning in disgrace but maybe hadn't done anything wrong. In other words, *Absence of Malice* (1981) had us right where director Sydney Pollack wanted us.

Actor Wilford Brimley was perfectly cast. He was Assistant U.S. Attorney General James Wells, and he was asking his investigator a critical question:

"What'd you figure you'd do after government service, Elliot?"

Elliott Rosen, played by actor Bob Balaban, replied, *"I'm not quitting."*

"You ain't no presidential appointee, Elliott. One that hired you is me. You got 30 days."

Ahh, the old "you've got 30 days" firing. This, of course, was a distinct softening from "draw your pay," which, during the early factory years, had been the standard. Today, many employers fear their employees, their employees' attorneys, and investigations by the Department of Justice or myriad other organizations—such that we have lost sight of the role and rule of employees.

EMPLOYEES DO THE WORK
THAT MAKES YOU RICH.

The purpose of a business is to make a profit. It says so in the early pages of the first chapter of pretty much every Introduction to Business college textbook. And, of course, it is. If you have a different purpose, you likely don't have a business. To make a profit—it has a nice sound to it. And unless you are the only employee, that profit is made by other people. Your "people," who we know as employees.

Quite simply, in every business it is the employees who make the investors rich. Don't be confused and believe that it is the customers. Of course the customers are the ones in the exchange—their money for our product or service, but that is only happening because of our people. It is a good arrangement as they (the employees) are provided with work, presumably salary and sometimes benefits, from minimum-wagers to skilled labor, middle management on up. They make up our national workforce, and their earnings, when spent and rolled over in communities, "feed the beast" that is our economy.

But workers are two distinct tales in most of our businesses. One tale, on the downside, starts with the "yellow suiters," meaning those who are so toxic we need protective gear to get rid of them.* What is interesting about toxic workers is that they often seem to be pretty good workers; they just negatively affect those around them. Ultimately, we must close our eyes to the good aspects of their work and fire them. Then the employee scale rolls up to those who are not toxic but just uninspired, and put in their time and do their work uninspired.

The other tale is the story about workers who like their work, like the company, maybe like us, and are doing the work that makes us "rich." A LinkedIn study (July 27, 2016) reported that fully half of all workers were satisfied with their jobs, the highest level in a decade. Trending up in satisfaction is always good. But before we celebrate too much, let's look at that number—half, 50 percent—are satisfied with their jobs. That leaves an equal number dissatisfied. That is not a good number.

Maybe it's just that workers can't be satisfied, or that we in management always pay them poorly and take advantage of them. People may have lost their desire to work. But those of us in management push numbers every day, and if we can have 50 percent satisfied, then we can have 60 percent or 70 percent. The number is not a scientific law. And there are actions that increase worker satisfaction.

In Hard Truth #6, "Pay," I offer a warning about expecting pay to gain much worker loyalty for you. But while it is important to pay workers competitively, it is even more important to treat them *with* importance. When they are assembling or fabricating on the factory floor, they are of utmost importance. When they are working the phones and gaining clients or closing a deal, they are of utmost importance. And when they greet a customer coming into your store or firm, they are of utmost importance. They are not working to make us rich; they are working because work is what they do and they are prideful of it.

But do not confuse their good work and pride in it as an endorsement of you, or a commitment to loyalty, or an indication they are your friend. These are dangerous conceits to cultivate and will invariably lead to disappointment. Few workers today "ride for the brand." We have pretty much lost those words and that ethic in our stylish new civilization.

Today we must consider our employees like a professional football coach considers his starting lineup. These are the
players he has, and these are the ones he will put on the field
at game time. They stand together in frigid weather, and the
players sacrifice their bodies for trophies and pay. It is a broth-
erhood. But when a better player is available, the coach releases
and signs, cuts and drafts. It is a business designed to make a
profit.

Myriad laws may make our business less quick and less mo-
bile with employees than in the business of the NFL, but when
we are advantaged to do so we must also make cuts, sometimes
of our "friends." And then our best strategy is to fire fast. Before
"friendship" muddles our thinking and strategy, and before new
workers think they have "homestead" rights on a particular job.

So, we build our workforce and maintain it, one worker at
a time. Every morning when we open our doors, or when the
new shift rotates into the call center, those are the best and most
important employees we have, at that moment. We should treat
them like it.

Employees (people) know that we cannot and will not pay
them more than we can, nor more than what is competitive
in a given field. What they want is dignity and respect for the
work they do. It is instructive, as this book is being written, to
have just observed the presidential election of 2016, and the
transition events following the election of President Trump. He
is a billionaire, yet he has an uncanny connection with many
working men and women. He is so far distanced from their
lives, yet they see him as one who understands them and their
daily toil and work. Work that he has never done.

Trump's words and tone are of utmost respect when he
talks about factory workers or coal miners. This from a man
who has not regularly voiced respect for many things. But on

this channel that he seems to have with workers, he plays it near perfectly. There is something to learn from that.

For, in addition to all of our other work, we as managers must put forth our best efforts to reinforce our worker in her or his work. To let them know we recognize their efforts. To see them on the shop floor and at our construction sites. And to sometimes help. The best example of this continues to be restaurant managers. The good ones are amazing to watch. When the restaurant is busy, you will see the manager move quickly to seat patrons, fill iced tea glasses, and bus tables. Not at all their job, except for when it is, and the good ones do it well. They won't do it for long periods at a time, but they make the statement and show that they see their workers are stretched. Everyone steps faster. They may not have had the time to help out, but in managing their 168-hour week (see Hard Truth #5) they make time, and reap the reward later.

Yes, the hard truth is that our employees will always be among our biggest satisfiers and sometimes our biggest disappointment. They work for *us* and we owe them dignity, respect, eye contact, high fives, shoulder pats, time when they need it, and sometimes help.

HARD TRUTH #15:

YOU MAY HAVE TO FIRE THEM TOMORROW, BUT TODAY THEY WORK FOR YOU AND YOU MUST TREAT THEM WELL.

*"Hazard Warning: The Unacceptable Cost of Toxic Workers" by Roberta Holland, HBSWk, January 20, 2016.

HARD TRUTH #16

INFLUENCE

If not power, then influence

———

From the moment I first heard Zig Ziglar speak, I knew I wanted to be a motivational speaker. I loved his positive life message and especially his rapid-fire Southern sing-song way of speaking. I could do that. And so I did. I developed several topics with some good life messages and adequate humor, and began to advertise. Gigs came, and I had some success over the years. Keynote, workshop, and dinner speaking supplemented my consulting practice, and I was soon well-traveled and decently paid.

But, as I am wont to do, I jumped into my work. And the more I studied motivation, the more I realized I was not a motivational speaker. I didn't motivate anyone. Maybe I was entertaining, but likely of very little value beyond that. I found myself in violation of my own beliefs and teachings in authenticity (see Hard Truth #1). Consulting and training could stay, but so-called "motivational" speaking had to go.

Thus began my internal war between motivation and influence. I had learned that people must develop their own motive for action, unless they are responding to a large dose of power (see Hard Truth #11), and even then, life has choices. But I thought if I could simply inspire them enough to be influential, they would develop the motivation to improve their lives and outlook. Suddenly a new player was on the scene—inspire—a.k.a. "inspiration."

My work became more murky as I then had three players to contend with and find perfect spots for in my work—influence, inspiration, and motivation. There are multiple definitions for each, and overlaps of definitions are easily found, but these words are not one and the same.

As providence would have it, as I was navigating through these three words and their meanings, I received from my son and daughter-in-law, Robert Cialdini's national bestseller, *Influence: The Psychology of Persuasion* (Harper, 2007). It is truly the near single-source authoritative writing on influence and should have been in my professional library, but somehow was not. Once I had read it, I then understood the power of influence.

In the leadership trade, as parents, business managers, leaders, and owners, and as civic or "movement" leaders, we attempt to influence in order to encourage a result. We don't have to attempt to influence as long as we are okay with results that differ from what we want, or if we don't care to be leaders. But then, let's be honest about our position and sit out the criticism part.

SPEND POWER OR EXERT INFLUENCE—WHICHEVER IS MORE CERTAIN.

But for most of us, influence is what we are doing whenever we are not exerting power. Power can be immediate. Power can be used without warning. Power can be subtle, but it can also be by-damn-now! Influence invariably happens over time. And for us to be influential with our family, community, or work constituent groups and teams, we must lay the groundwork.

Influence does not appear magically from flat seas. As leaders, we understand that from day one we are working to increase our sphere of influence. We begin with a plan (see Hard Truth #12, "Strategy") and we execute (intentionally) by the minute with every comment and move we make (see Hard Truth #7, "Intentionality"). If we are not making comments or taking actions for the purpose of influencing others, then why are we doing them at all? We are doing the work, so why not collect our influence every time we pass "Go"? Yet, unlike the board game Monopoly, our work and influence collecting is not automatic and does not rely on rolling the dice. No, all of leadership is intentional, and influence-building efforts must be more than the equivalent of a conference dinner speaker, and can never be relegated (metaphorically)—like my speaking experiences—to entertainment.

Simple daily repartee with our assistant or a coworker should be for a purpose. A major failing of leaders of all sorts is their belief that employees are easily on board with them. They are not, and for good reason. First, whatever the issue, you as the manager or leader have thought about it, read about it, written about it, discussed it, ruminated on it while jogging or biking, and/or otherwise had six or seven interactions with it. You know it and own it. One good briefing, memo, or policy writing distributed to your staff will not bring them to the level of understanding that you have. You must teach in order to influence.

You must also gain and control "colonies" in your unit and organization to increase your influence. Just like the British Empire of old, which was a small country but had a world of influence due to its colonies around the globe. As they lost their colonies, they similarly lost their influence.

The wise leader desiring to be influential establishes "colonies" one person, one employee at a time. First, with simple and ordinary conversation. Then, with small tidbits of tactical conversation. The influence relationship has begun. The leader then follows with a small business-related favor, and with reciprocity it is returned. By the time the leader needs the support of the employee, said employee is well-briefed on the subject or strategy, has trust and relationship with the leader, and thus has already bought in. That will gain the buy-in of others.

This is how influence is cultivated and grown in organizations. One employee at a time, just like colonies are established. It goes without saying that selecting your employees who will become colonies is a decidedly strategic decision, an intentional choice. Colonies take time. Colonies take work. But colonies will give you influence and, in turn, power over time.

Influence is by far the older brother or sister of inspiration or motivation. It can be built strategically, and controlled reciprocally, by leaders desirous enough to invest efforts and strategy to that end.

HARD TRUTH #16:

YOU EITHER HAVE INFLUENCE
WITH YOUR TEAM OR YOU ARE
A FIGUREHEAD.

CONFLICT

Only 15 percent of workers like how conflict is handled

———

He stormed into my office, already talking fast and angrily. "I am so tired of Jill. She undercuts me at every turn, takes credit for my work, and gives unsolicited advice to my clients. I've had it!"

"Good morning, Don," I said, looking up. "Have a seat."

Over the next half hour, we talked about what had Don so upset. It was a coworker. As I listened and let Don relate Jill's sins, making a few notes, I determined that Don had a point. Jill had indeed crossed the line a time or two, and I would visit with her. Other accusations were more in the line of Don's emotions piling on to the good woman who was generally a good employee.

When Don finished, I simply said, "I get it. I'll fire Jill today."

Don started, and stammered, "I don't want you to fire her."

"Then what do you want?"

"I want her to not overstep into my work and my clients."

"I understand," I said. "I will visit with Jill today. But first, walk with me."

We got up and left my office, walked past my assistant's desk, and out into the lobby of our complex. I pointed to a framed document on the wall. Don suddenly knew what was coming. It was our office "Relationship Agreement," crafted by the staff (not by me) and signed by all, including me. It read:

We commit that clients are our primary objective.
We value and support teamwork and collegiality.
We respect one another.
We model positive attitudes and relationships.

"How'd we do?" I asked Don. He sighed. "I know, I should have visited with Jill rather than tattling to you."

"Why?" I asked. "You know you can always come to me, just like you did."

"Yes, but it would have been more respectful and probably helped our relationship rather than tattle and expect you to fix it."

"Exactly." I smiled. "So, did Jill not have the clients at heart?"

"No, she did."

"And did her advice adversely affect them?"

"No, she gave them good advice. She knows what she is doing."

"So her mistake was in not referring them to you, or checking with you first?"

"Yes."

"I understand. Don, I will visit with Jill about this today. And you will visit with her sometime after, right?"

"Right."

"You're a good man."

And so he was, and so was Jill a good person and employee. But conflicts are part of the workplace. I had not fooled myself into thinking that forcing them to write a so-called "Relationship Agreement" would end conflicts. It simply gave me a better tool and foundation to teach them how to solve conflicts at the core and maintain good working relationships.

I visited with Jill, and she understood she had not shown respect to Don by seemingly "poaching" his clients. I also made it clear that I expected her to not resent Don coming to me and tattling. We are "clients first," I reminded her, and if we squabble amongst ourselves that can affect our clients. She understood, and understood that Don would be visiting her soon, if she did not get down the hall to see him first. It was good. Problem solved. For today.

Conflicts in organizations are common as mud, and can actually be healthy for working relationships. But we need to be ready to teach off of conflicts and use them to strengthen our team. Meanwhile, research shows that only 15 percent of employees report being satisfied with how their employers handle conflict or incivility in the workplace.* That's a very poor number and an indictment of us—the managers, the leadership. We should be better.

First, understand that if there is no conflict in a workplace it is because we have hired passive losers, none of whom have ambition or embrace the mission and goals of our company. Business is competitive, and competitive people compete. That's what feeds the beast that we hope is our growing enterprise and economy.

Gary Kubiak, former coach of the Denver Broncos professional football team, responded after a game to media questions about a pushing episode between two players. "I tell our players that we battle together, we do not battle each other." Fair enough, yet every sports fan watching knew he was privately pleased that a star player cared enough about winning to correct a rookie. It didn't require a coach to make the point.

Yes, competition can breed conflict, but management and leadership hold the team together. And when we do need to address it, it's not the conflict we address, it's the chip or hole in our agreement that requires repair.

In almost any conflict situation that has occurred, we will have more common agreement with those we are momentarily in conflict with than things we disagree on. As a leader, you need to make that vivid. To do so, pick up a legal pad or go to a planning whiteboard with a marker and draw a vertical line down the middle. Then label one side "Agree" and the other side "Disagree."

Start with the "Agree" side and begin to list what we all can agree on. Let's consider Don and Jill, although their conflict never needed to come to this process. The conversation would go something like this:

> *Can we agree that we are a **"clients first"** company?* (Yes? Write "clients first" on the Agree side)

> *Can we agree that we should **support each other** for the good of the company and ourselves?* (Write "support each other")

> *Can we agree that we all want to **maximize our earnings** through our client representation?* (Same process)

> *Can we agree that the three of us are **good and decent people**?*

*Can we agree that we have **a process of client priority** among our team?*

*Can we agree that we all signed the **Relationship Agreement** that hangs in our lobby?*

Can we agree…

And so on.

There you see it. As we pile on the agreements we have, our conflicts or disagreements begin to shrink in comparison. Believe it or not, this is how Congress works. We think of them as always in conflict and gridlocked, but in reality, their core agreements on our way of government and our freedoms outweigh the arguments on the floor that we see. Notice how a member is recognized to speak: *"The Chair recognizes the gentleman from Tennessee."* This is a body steeped in traditions of major undergirding <u>agreement</u> that always outweighs the current argument. Some countries solve legislative conflicts with armies and tanks, but in the greatest republic in the world, we solve it by managing (well) our most valued agreements.

QUIT FIGHTING THE WEEDS AND CONCENTRATE ON GROWING YOUR GRASS.

So, after we work through our list of agreements, we do the same on the "Disagree" side. It will be a shorter list, and a good manager or leader will work the long list to ultimately dissolve the short one and strengthen the employees' agreement at the same time. We teach authentically (see Hard Truth #1) and plant and reinforce with intentionality (see Hard Truth #7) those core agreements we want them to take away. It is managing those agreements and keeping them nourished that will weed out many, if not most, conflicts.

We tend to get better at that which we work on the most. Thus it is that managers who pride themselves for tackling conflict will be pretty good conflict fighters. But is that what we want in our leaders? Days spent playing Whac-a-Mole? Would it not be better to strengthen our agreements, our commitments, our sameness, and teamwork? Winners go for the latter.

HARD TRUTH #17:

CONFLICT RESOLUTION IS FOR LOSERS. EMBRACE CONFLICT, AND MANAGE YOUR AGREEMENTS.

*Christine Porath, *Harvard Business Review* (April 2016)

HARD TRUTH #18

IMAGE

You are who they think you are

———

She owned the room. She was well-dressed in navy slacks, a white lace cuffed blouse, wide patent black belt, red jacket, and patent leather black heels. It was her meeting, a training she was conducting for about 50 state employees who had traveled to the state capital, as she was a department head in a large agency. The training was going well, and she was a very good trainer. I sat second chair in the training and was both observing and occasionally helping with materials. My part in the training would come later. And then, a visitor.

Into the room walked the agency head and the trainer's boss. Not my boss, I was a contractor—but next to the governor, one of the most powerful people in the state. Everyone turned to look, and I believe I alone saw the subtle metamorphosis take place. The director was also wearing a red jacket, but her jacket magically slid off and over an empty chair with a minimum of movement as the trainer moved across the room to welcome her boss who had come to see the training. A skillful legerdemain. One woman in the room with a red jacket—and it would be the ranking one.

I doubt the director noticed the little theater that played out to her benefit, or appreciated the image awareness of a loyalist. But she certainly would understand the importance of image in an image-driven world. All politicians do. Business leaders do too—*if* they want to compete and win.

The modern western world is about as unfair a place to earn a living in management as has existed in history. This, in spite of protections for those with disabilities and guaranteed equality for women and minorities. The problem is "image" and what we "know" leaders to look like.

It is, of course, an absurd statement that we "know" what leaders look like. It is inherently racist, sexist, and any other "-ist." Yet it is decidedly mammalian to look to the male, and the largest one at that, for leadership. It is also perpetuated in our literature, historical and novels, and the movie industry— at least that of my developmental youth. From 17th-century Japan seeking 6-foot-plus-tall field generals so they were easily spotted in the field, to movies about the American West starring 6-foot-4-inch John Wayne, and a host of others—Gary Cooper, Charlton Heston, Burt Lancaster, and Gregory Peck— all 6-foot-2 or taller. Of course, back then, women and minorities were not (generally) considered for leadership positions.

Roll forward the mythical West to the very real industrial giant the United States was becoming in the early 1900s. A University of Chicago accounting professor founded McKinsey & Company in 1926. The era of 6-foot-tall Harvard-educated management and leadership consultants with plain socks was born. Yes, socks, and plain ones.

Marvin Bower didn't create James O. McKinsey's company, but he knew how to make it great, effectively inventing the consulting business. Enter the *image* of success. Bower's McKinsey consultants were smarter than many (Harvard), taller than most (6-foot), and better-dressed than their clients. From the moment they entered a company's headquarters until their arrival at the executive suites, they exuded "leadership."

Back to the socks...Bower required field consultants to wear long socks, preferably with garters, and disallowed argyles or other bright patterns. His reasoning? In meetings, if people are looking at your hairy legs or the patterns on your socks, then they are not focusing or listening to what you are saying. That is a very interesting point, and one whose relevance is still with us today. Unshined shoes speak to an unintentional life (see Hard Truth #7), and lost contracts.

What do we want our clothing to do for us? Mark Twain famously said, "Of course clothes make the man. Naked people have little influence on society." Point taken. But to what extent do clothing or size affect the perception and image of our leadership, and how do we use that to our advantage? Again, the world here is not at all fair.

In 2006, television news personality Katie Couric was assigned as evening news anchor at CBS, making history as the first woman to serve in that position at that network. She had an uneventful first night on air, but some of the reviews following focused on her wearing a white jacket after Labor Day. A fashion no-no for women of culture. Could Couric not have known? That act is credited by some with damaging Couric's image, and thus her credibility as an evening news anchor. She never gained strong ratings in the position.

We can argue the absurdity and even sexism of this criticism, but it was mostly female reviewers who found her wanting. Fast forward to 2014 and (U.S.) President Obama went on air to give a major policy speech with the world watching. He wore a beige suit, and although it was summer, the suit (of course) was simply inexcusable for a U.S. President. The critics, including some from Congress, hit him hard over the weakened image he portrayed. Beige simply is not the color of global leadership.

And thus it is an image-driven world, with YouTube, Facebook, and countless other opportunities for people to see us either as weak, or strong and "tall in the saddle." Silly, of course, but impactful to our careers. Which is not at all silly. The psychology world believes as much. Aaron W. Lukaszewski, an Oklahoma State University psychology professor, and his multi-university study team published "The Role of Physical Formidability in Human Social Status Allocation," a study that found that both men and women associate the appearance of physical strength—and to some extent, height—with leadership qualities and higher status.

BEING AN IMAGE DENIER WILL GET YOU BEAT.

Few of us can heighten ourselves, but we can positively enhance our image, partly with skill and partly with physicality. When I work with business students or clients, they will ask how to overcome their body type or lack of height. First, we agree that it is a silly world where those factors are important or even noticed. But being an image denier will get you beat in today's image-conscious world. The short answer I give them is to groom better, dress better, speak better, and have better posture. Improve your manners and business etiquette—pick up Barbara Pachter's excellent book, *The Essentials of Business Etiquette: How to Greet, Eat, and Tweet Your Way to Success.* Consider a career coach or executive coach to help you move the needle of your professional image. The next answer to my students and clients is to take stock of their physical fitness and make improvements there, if needed. But regardless, polish the image. And polish your shoes.

The hard truth is that it is not just our work competence alone that propels us in our company or organization. That would be true in a more perfect world. But we are "two" and not one—we are our competence as an accountant, investor, engineer, or manager, and we are also an image in the eyes of others. We must strategically manage both unless we are totally independent and own the company, and rumpled is okay. Clothing and image.

We must, of course, be competent in our work. But quiet competence can get you overlooked. You need to look like the leader to be the leader. Aili McConnon, writing for the Wall Street Journal (Oct. 3, 2016) reminds us that leaders are "always on display." And she takes us through the nonverbal cues that will speak volumes of our leadership, cues such as eye contact, a ready smile, strong posture, and more. Exactly. People notice. Why else in 2016 is she writing this for the *Wall Street Journal*?

Image will not turn a loser into a leader, though, any more than a "swoosh" symbol will make Nike a good shoe. But once established, Nike guards the reputation and placement of its (branding) swoosh far more than any individual product. The swoosh is the company. And so it is with us. Good work, strong leadership, and an image that propels both—all are necessary in today's image-driven world. But only if we care to win.

HARD TRUTH #18:

YOUR IMAGE CAN TAKE
YOU FARTHER—OR NOT—THAN
YOUR GOOD WORK ALONE.

CONCLUSION

Following the "Hard Truths" makes
hard work better, not easier

———

My phone would ring, and a good friend or colleague would ask, "Mike, can you go to coffee? I want to bounce something off of you." Me? Of course I can go to coffee. I love coffee—hot, dark roasted and toasted, smoky, and strong enough to eat through the cup. There is none better than in the burn-your-lips metal canteen cups from the army, boiled over Sterno, but the time and place likely contributed to that.

So my friend would come by, and we would go to coffee. I knew what he or she wanted, and it wasn't to let me in on a special investment deal. They had a problem and needed to pitch it to someone. I had become sort of a catcher...

And so, *Hard Truths*. I am by no means the best or most experienced manager or leader in the business. I am a social scientist, and I have worked to become a student of the "game." As such, probably my most important discovery is that management and leadership are too important of responsibilities to execute with make-it-up-on-the-fly decisions. You need a playbook you believe in, and the stones to execute your playbook flawlessly and intentionally.

Over coffee, I would visit with my friend or colleague, and they would lay out a situation that was challenging them. When they were done, I would ask them what they believed about the situation, the background, the options, the people involved, the potential, and the chance of blowback. Then we would drill down to the core problem, and I would question their belief system related to it. Sometimes they didn't have one…they simply tried to apply a strategy to the situation. I told them, as I have related in Chapter 12 (Strategy), that they were playing a loser's game.

Strategy without a theory or philosophy behind it is a coin toss. It is akin to a random decision without intentionality behind it (see Hard Truth #7). What do you believe? And what do you expect to happen from your decision or action? That is the core to the making of a good manager or leader. Executing based upon bedrock beliefs, not whims.

The previous paragraph notwithstanding, I do not mean that judgment and "snap" decisions are useless. Yes, there are times when we need to decide fast, act fast, and move fast. My point is that, in those times, it is even more critical to be grounded in our playbook and to act with intentionality.

LIVE AUTHENTICALLY AND ACT INTENTIONALLY.

And that is what I encourage and coach over coffee, with friends and with clients. This book is a conversation, a culmination of years of study and experience, and lots of coffee. The bottom line of *Hard Truths,* the short story, is found in a combination of Hard Truths #1 and #7; if you take nothing else from the book, being authentic by living an authentic life, and living and working intentionally, will serve you well.

It is my hope that you have enjoyed *Hard Truths,* and find at least some of the lessons useful to you and your management and leadership team. I am quite certain they should each have their own copy.

Lead on!

FINAL HARD TRUTH:

LEADERSHIP IS PLANNED
AND PURPOSEFUL ACTION
BY PREPARED AND
INTENTIONAL PEOPLE.

REFERENCES

BOOKS

Cialdini, R.B. (2007). *Influence: The psychology of persuasion.* New York, NY: HarperCollins.

Covey, S.R. (1989). *The 7 habits of highly effective people.* New York, NY: Fireside/Simon and Schuster.

Duckworth. A. (2016). *Grit: The power of passion and perseverance.* New York, NY: Scribner.

Frankl, V. (1946, 1997). *Man's search for meaning.* Boston, MA: Beacon Press.

French, J. & Raven, B. (1959). *The bases of social power.* In Forsyth, D. R. (2010, 2006). Group Dynamics. Boston, MA: Cengage Learning.

George, B. (2003). *Authentic Leadership.* San Francisco, CA: Jossey-Bass.

Greene, R. (1998). *The 48 laws of power.* New York, NY: Penguin Books.

Gunther-McGrath, R. (2013). *The end of competitive advantage.* Watertown, MA: Harvard Business Publishing.

Herzberg, F. (1959). *The motivation to work.* New York, NY: John Wiley.

Morgan, F.E. (1992). *Living the martial way.* Ft. Lee, NJ: Barricade Books.

Musashi, M. (2004). *The complete book of five rings.* Boston, MA: Shambhala Publishing.

Pachter, B. (2013). *The essentials of business etiquette: How to greet, eat, and tweet your way to success.* Columbus, OH: McGraw-Hill Education.

Ruiz, D.M. (1997). *The four agreements.* San Rafael, CA: Amber-Allen Publishing.

Sandberg, S. (2013). *Lean in: Women, work and the will to lead.* New York, NY: Borzoi-Knopf Publishing.

JOURNALS

Chafkin, M. (2016, August 4). Bloomberg Businessweek, *Yahoo's Marissa Mayer on selling a company while trying to turn it around.* New York, NY: Bloomberg L.P.

Goleman, D. (2013, Dec.). Harvard Business Review, *The focused leader.* Watertown, MA: Harvard Business Publishing.

Hammond, H. & Aneiro, M., et. al. (2004, Oct.). Fast Company, *Balance is bunk!* New York, NY: Mansueto Publications.

Ibarra, H. (2015, Jan.-Feb.). Harvard Business Review, *The authenticity paradox*. Watertown, MA: Harvard Business Publishing.

Ignatius, A. (ed.) (2015, Dec.). Harvard Business Review, *Compensation: Straight talk about pay*. Watertown, MA: Harvard Business Publishing.

Lukaszewski, A., Simmons, Z. et. al. (2014, Dec.). Journal of Personal and Social Psychology, *The role of physical formidability in human social status allocation*. Washington, D.C.: American Psychological Association.

Peters, T. (2001, March). Fast Company, *Leaders love the mess*. New York, NY: Mansueto Publications.

Porath, C. (2016, April). Harvard Business Review. *Managing yourself: An antidote to incivility*. Watertown, MA: Harvard Business Publishing.

Weimer, M. (2012, Sept.). Faculty Focus, *Students think they can multitask. Here's proof they can't*. Madison, WI: Magna Publications.

Zenger, T. (2013, June). Harvard Business Review. *What is the theory of your firm?* Watertown, MA: Harvard Business Publishing.

NEWSPAPERS

Ariely, D. (2016, Feb. 23). The Wall Street Journal, *Would a shorter workday mean less wasted time?* Manhattan, NY: News Corp.

McConnon. A. (2016, Oct 3). The Wall Street Journal,
    To be a leader watch your body language. Manhattan, NY:
    News Corp.

ONLINE
Dowd-Higgins, C. (2015, July 8). Huffington Post, *Balance is
    bunk: Realistic work/life integration strategies.*

Holland, R. (2016, Jan. 20). HBSWk.com, *Hazard warning:
    The unacceptable cost of toxic workers.* Watertown, MA:
    Harvard Business Publications.

Moseley, M. (2016, July 27). Linkedin.com, *50 percent of
    workers dislike their jobs.* Mountain View, CA: LinkedIn.

Urbandictionary.com (1999). Peckham, A, (ed.) Crowd
    sourced.

MOVIES
Absence of Malice. Pollack, C. (Dir.) (1981). Culver City, CA:
    Columbia Pictures.

Miami Vice. Mann, M. (Dir.) (2006). University City, CA:
    Universal Studios.

Hombre. Ritt, M. (Dir.) (1967). Century City, CA: 20th
    Century Fox.

Michael Tomlin is a writer, leadership and marketing consultant and trainer, and political messaging advisor. He has lectured in London, taught in Taiwan, and held leadership seminars on a cruise ship. His 40-plus-year career has traveled him to over 40 states, speaking, teaching, and training. He also served as a professor of business and professor of education, and as a college dean. Mike especially enjoys working with Chambers of Commerce and Small Business Development Centers to empower their members and constituents. He holds a doctorate from the University of Wyoming. He served both active and reserve assignments in the United States Army Special Forces and attained the rank of Major.

You can contact Mike at www.michaeltomlin.me.

elevate
publishing

**DELIVERING TRANSFORMATIVE MESSAGES
TO THE WORLD**

Visit www.elevatepub.com for our latest offerings.

NO TREES WERE HARMED IN THE MAKING OF THIS BOOK.

OK, so a few did make the ultimate sacrifice.

In order to steward our environment, we are partnered with *Plant With Purpose*, to plant a tree for every tree that paid the price for the printing of this book.

To learn more, visit www.elevatepub.com/about